First, let me say bc

be using a lot of the tips and tricks we've learned. That said, I'll commence with my thoughts:

I loved the section on asset vs. liability - sure puts things into a different perspective. And, definitely makes me think twice about another car loan any time soon. (This is why the car loan in #6 is perfect for me.)

Loved the suggestion about opening â bank account w/debit card vs. using a credit card. Chris and I have a card with a decent balance for emergencies that we only use enough to keep active. We're going to transition that to a bank account. :)

We both liked all the worksheets that went along with each chapter. What a great way to keep track of things and really review what we learned as we went through the book. Also, like most people we'd never really put a lot of it on paper in one place and/or one time. Very interesting to see.

We both think the book was done in a very positive way - shows the pros and cons of a lot of things - with good examples allowing people to make the decisions they need. It's not a "this is right, this is wrong" scenario, but more of a learning and self discovery process. It shows ways to make small changes with big impact and then ways to magnify that when you're ready.

It give us a lot to think about - both financially and personally. It helped us gain perspective on a lot of areas that we might have otherwise kept to ourselves. We always thought we were a team when it came to our finances, but this showed us that there are some things one wants that the other does not and vice versa. It's been a great jumping off point for us to start to share more of our hopes and dreams for the future - immediate and long term.

Well done my friend, well done. We wish you much success with this and can't wait to see it take off and change the lives of others as it's done for us.

—Chris & Michele

The information presented was very informative, real and presented in a very honest way. It helped me see a real way to change my habits and mind set around my financial health as well as become one with my spouse. We're both very excited about the plan of action we can take away as a result of reading Consider the Ant. Before reading, our view of money and how God wants us to succeed was very superficial. Now, thanks to Consider the Ant, we have a grasp on where to start change in our financial lives. Thank you.

—Brian & Jennifer

Consider the Ant is full of ancient but practical wisdom to help build financial certainty in the most uncertain times. With Biblical references throughout, Joshua Christensen shows exactly how to enjoy abundance right now, with freedom from fear, so we can bless those around us. Truly, book is a Winner!

—Gina Parris
Founder,
Built To Win Coaching
Tullahoma, TN

Consider the ANT

Consider the ANT

3 KEYS TO BIBLICAL PROSPERITY

Joshua Christensen

Tate Publishing & *Enterprises*

Consider the Ant

Published by Tate Publishing & Enterprises, LLC
127 E. Trade Center Terrace | Mustang, Oklahoma 73064 USA
1.888.361.9473 | www.tatepublishing.com

Tate Publishing is committed to excellence in the publishing industry. The company reflects the philosophy established by the founders, based on Psalm 68:11,
"The Lord gave the word and great was the company of those who published it."

Cover design by Amber Gulilat
Interior design by Nathan Harmony

Published in the United States of America

ISBN: 978-1-61663-196-3
Business & Economics: Personal Finance: General
10.04.06

Dedication

This book is dedicated to the love of my life, my incredible bride. She is my gift from the Lord whom I diligently hope to honor in all I do. She is my support, my biggest fan, my inspiration, and my love. For years, Belinda has stood quietly by my side with an inner strength that only comes from the Lord. Thank you for being my wife, my love, and my best friend.

Acknowledgments

To my two girls, Celia and Gabriela, who have patiently sat by, wanting so badly to play, but knew not to disturb me while I was busy writing. They are my joy and my inner warmth. To Steve Schmit, who many years ago studied the Bible with me and baptized me into my Lord, Jesus Christ. Steve, thank you for never giving up on me when I gave up on myself and when I gave up on the Lord. To Bill Moulden, who encouraged me and gently spurred me on many mornings over coffee, asking when I would write this book. To Kate Wilson, my coach, my mentor, my friend, who took a chance on me when I did not meet her criteria for a coaching student. Kate, you saw something in me and would not let me go. For your support, trust, honesty, direction, hope and love, thank you. To Jackson Barroso, my best friend and my brother. You have inspired me by your perseverance and dedication to your family while in pursuit of your dreams without abandon. Your drive and passion is contagious, and your belief in me is not without merit. To Luis Sanchez, who has shown me the power of friendship and the power of trust. You've trusted me with all of your financial matters to help you and your family grow and become better stewards. You've trusted me with loyalty and friendship. To the families who went through the book each week in our home as my "guinea pigs" while working through these issues: Matt and Hillary, Brian and Jennifer, Lindsey and Karina, Luis and Heather, Dan and Abby, and Keith and Lynn. To Keith and Lynn Rassmussen, who helped me with countless hours of editing and suggestions to strengthen this work for the greatest impact to the world. To all those whom I sent my first draft to, requesting feedback. Thank you for all of your valuable feedback and support. To Scott Cummings, for your belief, support, and suggestions as I worked through the pages of this book, calling me to live my teachings as a brother in Christ would and should do. To Jack Thompson, who took me in as a mentor, friend, and proof editor. You believed in me and took me in when you didn't know me and had nothing to gain from a relationship with me. You've exemplified a life of giving to others. Thank you. To my mom, Karen Christensen, who has always supported me and believed in me when no one else did. To my dad, Dean Christensen, who taught me about integrity, diligence, and how to provide for my family. To David Libby, who listened to countless hours of my rambling on about the book, as well as sharing your thoughts with me. To Alex Moghadam, who read and reread these pages and offered suggestions and support as I wrote. To Greg and Patty Sofio, who have shown true generosity, true friendship, and true living as you've shared so much with me from the abundance God has blessed you with. I've been truly blessed with so many wonderful people in my life who have believed in me and loved me through this work. I also would like to acknowledge all of my clients over the years, who have been great teachers and students of mine, as you've all been loyal to me regardless of where my feet may have taken me. Most of all, I want to thank God for never giving up on teaching me the lessons that my life needs to draw me closer to you. Thank you.

Table of Contents

Foreword

Money means so many different things to people. Some see it as an evil part of our society. Some see it as the hope in a lottery ticket. Others see it as a central theme in the struggles of their marriage. Before reading *Consider the Ant,* I want to suggest that you reflect on what money is for you. What prejudices do you carry regarding money? What has it meant or not meant in your life? I can assure you that if you will take this moment to consider all of the positive and negative views about money that you carry in your life before pressing forward through this book, you will find that it will touch you deeply for a better future.

Consider for a moment how much money is involved with our daily activities. To make a trip to the grocery store, we need money for our transportation (i.e. for our car payment, insurance, gas, and maintenance of our vehicle). When we get to the store, we need money to purchase our items. What about the store itself? The store needs money to operate. They need money to pay the electricity, staff employees, insurance, and a myriad of other overhead items. All the food manufacturers need money to provide the products for the store. All the other patrons of the store need money, just like you, to even be able to shop at the store—and so on, and so on, and so on. Can you see from this small example the impact money (mis)management has in our daily lives?

Now consider everything else that money touches in your life. It is, at times, beyond comprehension. I would argue that, next to the air we breathe, managing money is the single most important aspect of our lives that God has placed before us. Where would our missions in the church be without funding? How would the companies who produce Bibles produce anything without money to pay their bills? You see, most of us think about money as green pieces of paper with presidents that allow us to buy more and more stuff. Money is a much deeper part of our lives. It is a tool for bartering and managing the time, talents, and resources that God has put us in charge of on the Earth.

Who created us? Who created the resources on the Earth? Who created our means of using these resources? God, of course. That being true, then we have to accept that God is the creator of economic systems. He alone created the rules to good "fiscal stewardship." This understanding is what makes *Consider the Ant* such a powerful book. It asks you to set aside your prejudices regarding money. It asks you to recognize that the Creator of all things also created money. It asks you to go to him to be faithful stewards of his resources.

God has blessed Joshua Christensen with a life that has forced him to wrestle with these same questions and answers. Like so many of us, it is not easy to see these trials as blessings; but only through the life Joshua has lived is he able to relate to all of us concerning our fears, failures, and hopes regarding money. God will use *Consider the Ant* to bless you if you will let Him. Before proceeding, take a moment to pray. Ask God to reveal and set aside all the various biases you may be carrying regarding money so that you may be open to what He wants to share with you through *Consider the Ant*.

Blessings,

—J. Grant Magers
CEO
Moola Monsters, LLC
www.moolamonsters.com

Who Is Joshua Christensen?

First of all, if you're reading this book, thank you. I truly hope that the things I share here will help you find the path the Lord wants for your life.

So who am I? Great question.

I'll start answering that question by telling you that I am not someone defined by the things I've done—titles, degrees, or career choices. I can't say that I've always believed that. If you'd asked me this question a year ago when I started writing this book, I would have shared about my accomplishments, my relationships, my career, and my faith. However, during my writing, the Lord provided new direction and amazing revelations that radically changed the very fabric of my belief system. My hope is that you will find new revelations and new beliefs within these pages as I have.

So who am I? I am Joshua Christensen, son of Dean and Karen Christensen, born in Albert Lea, Minnesota in July of 1973. I tried to come a few months early; but thanks to quick thinking of the doctors and limited knowledge of premature birth in those days, I was able to hang on until the eighth month. Still a month early, I've often been described as somewhat impatient. We lived in a small Iowa border town.

Let me go back to describe a little of my heritage as you get to know me. My family history is that of farmers coming through the Great Depression and the European famines of the late 1800's. Ours was a story of struggle for the American dream as my great grandfather fought to come to America in the late 1880's to find a small farm where he could raise a family. After a few years, he was able to save enough to go back to Denmark for my great grandmother. Together, they raised thirteen children in Iowa. My grandfather, born in 1907, was the twelfth child in the group. He is truly one of my biggest heroes.

During the Depression, my grandpa Bill traveled all over Minnesota, North and South Dakota, and Iowa with his brother, looking for farm work to survive. At any opportunity, he would give up his shirt for his neighbor if that neighbor lacked. At eighty years old, my dad and my uncles finally convinced him to stop framing houses and come down from the roof. He was tough as nails. But Grandpa Bill raised my father, who passed on many of his great qualities to me.

Work hard and ask only what you can do for others, not what they can do for you. Pay yourself 10 percent and God 10 percent first before anything else. Do whatever it takes to provide for those you love. If you've got it to give, give generously. Don't withhold your time from someone who could use a little of it. If you don't have anything nice to say, don't say it. (Unfortunately, I've had to learn this one again as I've gotten older.) Protect your integrity. If you say you'll do it, do it. Make promises carefully, but keep them when you do. Don't forget to laugh and have fun along the way.

Great men gave me a good foundation. I departed from these teachings in my early adult life. I thought I knew a lot more than I actually do. What they say is true. The older I get, the less I know.

> Teach a youth about the way he should go; even when he is old he will not depart from it.
>
> Proverbs 22:6 (HCSB)

> Listen, my son, to your father's instruction, and don't reject your mother's teaching, for they will be a garland of grace on your head and a gold chain around your neck.
>
> Proverbs 1:8–9 (HCSB)

So, about me. We lived near my grandparents in Iowa until I was nine years old when a new job opportunity took us to Dallas, Texas. Mom and Dad struggled with money my entire childhood. We didn't miss any meals, but I was certainly reminded that "money does not grow on trees." I grew up watching Mom and Dad struggle. There were periods when Dad was on the strike line at the tire factory with no income. We traded in bottles and cans for the nickel or dime refunds.

We lived in rented houses or apartments from the time I was five. Mom and Dad split up while I was in sixth grade.

I didn't know who I wanted to live with, so I spent a few years bouncing back and forth. From age eleven, I felt very alone. Although I didn't pay the rent or provide the food, I felt like the cooking, cleaning, and laundry were my responsibility. We had a saying in our house around dinner time: "Fend for yourself." And that's what I learned.

Dad was working overtime to make ends meet. When he came home in the evening, he fell asleep in the rocking chair watching the news until he wandered into bed around 9:30 or 10:00. He worked hard to provide for us. Those were some lean years. Unfortunately, it wasn't until I was a father and husband that I understood what he was doing. During those years, I was angry and felt very alone and lost. I've grown to have an incredible respect for what my father did during those years.

I had to get Dad's signature on a waiver to allow me to work at age fifteen. I wanted badly to earn my own way, so I bagged groceries and worked as a cashier through my sophomore and junior years in high school. We didn't have a lot of money, and groceries were scarce at times, so I worked to have money for two school lunches and meals at my job. It was during those days that I declared to myself that my children would not know hunger. I'll explain more about that later.

As I ended high school, I was living with Mom, who went through a second divorce from my stepfather. We dealt with bankruptcy my senior year. Watching Mom cry every time the phone rang was challenging. I disengaged from society in many ways. I was angry that life was a struggle. Success was for special families who had all the "right" cards.

During my senior year, I started getting college packets. When I saw the tuition, I realized that there was no way I could afford to go to school, so I joined the navy—kind of a double-edged sword. I felt as though joining the navy would provide a way for college and "earn" my Dad's declaration of being proud of me. I was discharged after seven months and found myself lost again.

I spent the next five years wandering from job to job, in and out of college, getting into drugs, drinking heavily, and chasing girls. All I knew was to work and pay my bills on time, so I did.

I worked hard enough to cover my bills and to have enough for the next party. And party I did. I drank enough to black out three or four nights per week. I figured that if I could laugh and drink, I could forget about how miserable my life was shaping up to be. I had friends but felt alone. It was all superficial and temporary until 1995, when I moved to Albuquerque.

I was bartending at a local restaurant on New Year's Eve. My wife, whom I had not met yet, came in with some friends to meet before heading out to a church lock-in for New Year's. She invited me to church that night. I went with her the next Sunday and realized that three years earlier in Dallas, I was baptized in the same church where I didn't last more than three and a half months. We started dating exclusively eight months later. I am happy to say that we will celebrate eleven amazing years in June.

God reached out to save me from myself during some very dark years. I've had some amazing men help me figure a few things out along the way, to which I am very grateful. In

1996, God directed me to start my banking career as a teller at a large national bank here in Albuquerque. Inside of three and a half years, the doors opened to management. We were asked to give up everything and move to Las Cruces, NM to help with our church. When we put God first in our lives, promotions came about where no jobs existed.

As our little family grew, an opportunity at the bank redirected my career towards a banking specialty in the mortgage department. Again, I felt the Spirit moving me to a new adventure. That was in 2001.

Life was good. Belinda was able to come home and raise our children in 2002. I was so excited about God's provision in our lives. I thought, *Little ole me without a degree providing like this for our family.* We bought our first and second houses in those years. Times were very good.

Fast forward. By late 2007, I became very arrogant about the ways which God provided for my family. We had a decent amount saved in the bank. I was at a point where I was going to start investing in real estate with the money we saved. I made a decision in mid-2007 to try to go about my business on my own. I did not seek any advice or pray much about my decision. I believed that God prompted the move, but I acted very swiftly. What followed from the end of 2007, through all of 2008, and up to the current time is where I find myself in this journey God has provided.

I wrote this book in the midst of the lessons I'm about to share with you. The lessons from this book are tried and true. The results became some of the greatest lessons of my life. This book is a key to helping people avoid the mistakes I made along the way.

I truly believe that God provides opportunities to face trials of many kinds at our expense for the benefit of others later in life. I've been known to tell people, "What is happening to me is not for me." I believe God gives us lessons and helps us learn how to get through them so that we can help others in similar struggles as referenced in 2 Corinthians 1:3–7 (HCSB).

What I am about to share was the deepest seat of shame for me early last year. Today, however, it is one of the greatest blessings in my life. I can honestly say that I:

> Consider it a great joy, my brothers, whenever *I* experience various trials, knowing that the testing of *my* faith produces endurance. But endurance must do its complete work, so that *I* may be mature and complete, lacking nothing.
>
> James 1:2–4 (HCSB)

In August of 2007, the country was alerted to a problem that had been brewing for many years. Bank after bank after bank started to fail due to the rising number of foreclosures. The months that followed turned out to be one of the biggest economic crisis' during our lifetime. As you can imagine, my living was dependent upon writing mortgages. As business slowed to a trickle, we started using our savings to "weather the storm," supplementing our income with what we saved.

It was during those days that I started this book. I felt very proud of our ability to save for times such as these. Well, by February and March of 2008, the savings were gone, but income had not returned. It was time to start using our credit cards as a lifeline. I figured that we would be out of the mess by late spring, and I could pay off the cards. No. God had a different lesson for me.

In June, we started investing in real estate and secured our first investment property. We were extremely excited about it. Until July that is, when I realized that we had two houses, very low income, no savings, and no renter.

We decided to put our house up for sale and move into the smaller, more affordable investment property. Again, that all sounded good until the market fell further and our house wouldn't sell.

Fast forward eight months. As I write this, we are near completion of a liquidation bankruptcy, surrendering our home to the bank and wiping out over $120,000 in additional consumer debt. I will tell you that this has been absolutely the hardest year, financially, that we've ever faced. The funny thing is that while this has been difficult, we are extremely encouraged by God's love, support, and faith in us to prepare us for this message. He knew all along that we needed to experience the hardest times to strengthen us for the battle that lies ahead.

So I write all this to tell you that the amount of money, possessions, degrees, trophies, and relationships do not define who I am. No. All those things only have the value I assign to them.

I found myself doing things this year that tested my character, my dedication, and my commitment to family and to Jesus. I found myself in a position of lonely bitterness. I found myself dealing with the greatest fears of my adult life. I found myself relying on my own strength. I found myself crying out to God that I did not want my children to know hunger as I've known it.

At one point, I took on a job delivering pizza to make extra cash for my family and buy groceries if anything else.

I found myself learning the lesson of manna in the morning.

God led me on an awesome journey to reveal to me many things. Throughout this year, I've seen many of our friends and family struggle. I saw friends face bankruptcy and foreclosures. I counseled many clients who considered these avenues. All the while, we too were facing similar challenges.

This I know. God allowed me to face these trials so that I could learn the lessons that I am now writing about firsthand. In all these things, I have not lost my faith or my love because I know that his love for me is so much greater.

I stopped my work on this book in June 2008 when I realized where we were personally. I felt like a hypocrite. I can tell you honestly today that I am a champion. It would have been hypocritical for me to share these lessons without sharing my own shortcomings. I found that I have a great enemy (as do you) who does not want this information to get to you. He will not prevail, and this message will come to you.

These are hard lessons. This year, I realized that I am my father's son. I will fight for my family. I am a son of God, made in his image as a warrior. I am loved more than my shortcomings can begin to imagine. I am chosen for this purpose to teach others who are facing similar challenges.

In all this, I realized that I've been given so much and that much is expected of me. As you'll learn reading through these pages, I am at a point where I've been given a great deal and am now giving back.

I do not pretend to have all this figured out, but I know that we have an enemy among us who wants us to believe that we are entitled to a "good" life, which is provided by possessions. In this book, I hope you will realize that possessions have nothing to do with a "good, rich" life.

My kids often ask me if we are rich. And yes, this year, I have told my children and my wife that we are very rich. When 80 percent of the world went to bed hungry tonight, we had several meals today. I tucked my kids into bed while many kids do not have a bed to sleep in.

I was in a slight fender bender accident a few days ago and was reminded that life is short. Where and in what do you place value?

We are very rich. It's time that we all learn the lessons of fiscal stewardship. If you're reading this, it is because you've been richly blessed with the extra money to buy a book and the ability to read. It's time that we look for opportunities to serve others who are less fortunate as God intended.

I deeply believe that God wants us to have wealth that he can use to his glory not to our own. Pass this message along, and together we will glorify God in all he does. It is God's rich mercy that gives us the strength and power to overcome. To him be all honor and glory. May he bless you with peace that transcends all understanding.

My prayer is that this book will bless your financial life in such a powerful way as to change your future and that of your children and many generations to come.

—Joshua Christensen

Introduction and Orientation

> Go to the ant, you sluggard; consider its ways and be wise! It has no commander, no overseer or ruler, yet it stores its provisions in summer and gathers food at harvest. A little sleep a little slumber, a little folding of the hands to rest—and poverty will come on you like a bandit and scarcity like an armed man.
>
> Proverbs 6:6–11 (NIV)

Main Objective

What is fiscal stewardship? During the course of this book, you will learn about the Fiscal Stewardship Cycle.

You, like me, have probably read all kinds of different books on building wealth or getting rich. This is not one of those books. Below, I've outlined the main objectives of this work. In reading *Consider the Ant*, my goal for you is to:

1. Learn what it is God has given you.
2. Learn how God expects you to develop and grow that which you've been given to manage.
3. Learn how to give back from the abundance with which God has blessed you.
4. Learn basic knowledge of asset management.
5. Learn basic knowledge of liability management.
6. Learn basic knowledge of lifestyle management.
7. Learn basic knowledge of passing along legacy.

So what does God expect from us in terms of our financial wellbeing. We read so many passages about not serving two masters, God and money, in Matthew 6:24 and how the love of money is the root of all evil in 1 Timothy 6:10.

What are we supposed to think about money?

Does God want us to have money or to live with money?

Is money evil?

What are we supposed to do with money?

How is Satan using the modern-day economic boom of America to create slaves to the almighty dollar?

How has the rug been pulled out from under us with the current economic downturn affecting so many people around the world?

Do you remember when God created the earth and everything in it back in Genesis? Do you remember what he told Adam what his role was in this newly created earth? His role was to "work it and take care of it"

(Genesis 2:15, NIV). He was also in charge of naming all the animals, birds, fish, and reptiles. Whatever he named them, it was so. God gave Adam all authority on earth, with the exception of one boundary: do not eat from the tree of knowledge of good and evil.

Adam's primary role was one of being steward over that which God created. That stewardship was based on God's rules, which were very simple to follow. In fact, the rules were so simple that God only gave Adam one rule:

> And the Lord God commanded the man, "You are free to eat from any tree in the garden; but you must not eat from the tree of the knowledge of good and evil, for when you eat of it you will surely die."
>
> Genesis 2:16–17 (NIV)

When Adam chose not to obey, a curse was given, and the Lord God foreclosed on the garden of Eden (Genesis 3, NIV). Have you known anyone recently who lost their home, their dignity, their sense of pride, or their identity because of a foreclosure situation? In many of these cases, some fundamental financial rules were broken along the way to foreclosure. Foreclosure doesn't just happen overnight.

Who was it that convinced Eve to eat the fruit? That's right. Satan was right there, making the fruit very appealing to her. He filled her with fine-sounding arguments, making it seem like no big deal.

Have you ever purchased something on credit thinking that you'd pay it off at the end of the month, no big deal. "Pay now. Play now. Go ahead. You've earned it. You deserve it," he says. "You make enough to afford those payments. Look at how successful you've been. Show your friends your success. You need this. People in your position do this all the time."

Don't be fooled. He is slick and ever so subtle in his approach. Didn't he convince Eve by asking her, "Surely God didn't say you would die, did he?"

He is so good at what he does that he's got us telling each other the same lies so that he can relax. Don't we seek "advice" from those we trust who tell us everything will be okay if we can afford it? Be careful.

Interestingly enough, God later charged Noah with a similar task as Adam in the garden. He told Noah and his sons to, "Be fruitful and increase in number and fill the earth" (Genesis 9:1–4, NIV). They were given everything.

In the past, I've looked at being fruitful and increasing in number as one and the same—evangelism. If you break this down, these men were given charge of all the earth to care for the animals and the crops as well as increase in number. They were given the charge to grow that which they were given to oversee. Being fruitful is merely allowing the source to spring forth or overflow into more.

In those days, there were no monetary systems in place. The economy was strictly agricultural in nature. Eventually, man took God's created, gold and silver, and assigned value to it, making it the common bartering pieces. Along came the establishment of our current monetary system.

So, how does all of this apply to today? Well, we are in the very lineage of Adam and Noah, who were given this awesome responsibility to manage that which they were given.

Just as Adam was given a great responsibility in the garden and Noah was given the awesome responsibility to re-establish mankind, we too have been given much; and much will be expected from how we manage.

> From everyone who has been given much, much will be demanded; and from the one who has been entrusted with much, much more will be asked.
> Luke 12:48b (NIV)

Consider God's attitude about our stewardship in the parable of the ten minas. This parable outlines God's expectations of us to steward over that which he has entrusted to our care.

> While they were listening to this, he went on to tell them a parable, because he was near Jerusalem and the people thought that the kingdom of God was going to appear at once. He said: "A man of noble birth went to a distant country to have himself appointed king and then to return. So he called ten of his servants and gave them ten minas. 'Put this money to work,' he said, 'until I come back.' But his subjects hated him and sent a delegation after him to say, 'We don't want this man to be our king.' He was made king, however, and returned home. Then he sent for the servants to whom he had given the money, in order to find out what they had gained with it. The first one came and said, 'Sir, your mina has earned ten more.' 'Well done, my good servant!' his master replied. 'Because you have been trustworthy in a very small

> matter, take charge of ten cities.' The second came and said, 'Sir, your mina has earned five more.' His master answered, 'You take charge of five cities.' Then another servant came and said, 'Sir, here is your mina; I have kept it laid away in a piece of cloth. I was afraid of you, because you are a hard man. You take out what you did not put in and reap what you did not sow.' His master replied, 'I will judge you by your own words, you wicked servant! You knew, did you, that I am a hard man, taking out what I did not put in, and reaping what I did not sow? Why then didn't you put my money on deposit, so that when I came back, I could have collected it with interest?' Then he said to those standing by, 'Take his mina away from him and give it to the one who has ten minas.' 'Sir,' they said, 'he already has ten!' He replied, 'I tell you that to everyone who has, more will be given, but as for the one who has nothing, even what he has will be taken away. But those enemies of mine who did not want me to be king over them—bring them here and kill them in front of me.'"
>
> Luke 19:11–27 (NIV)

When the king was on his way out, he left ten minas (a mina was about three months' wages) with ten men. He expected each to manage the minas well. Upon his return, he saw that one of the men hid the minas and gave it back without interest. As a result, the king was furious at the man's lack of attention to the matter. The minas were removed, and the man was killed for his lack of loyalty to the king.

From this example and the example of Adam in the

garden or Noah and the townsmen, what can we conclude about how serious God is about our stewardship? He asked Adam and Eve to leave the garden with a curse. He then destroyed the earth and all but a few with the flood. In this parable, the king killed the man for his lack of loyalty.

Don't get me wrong. I don't want to paint a picture of an unloving, unmerciful God. However, if we do not take seriously the task God has entrusted to us, there are certainly consequences. Fiscal stewardship is not a matter to be taken lightly. God is serious with his trust; therefore, we must be serious in our management.

Because we've been given so much, we must diligently seek after the wisdom of God to understand how he wants us to be better stewards of his affairs and to ultimately bless others with it.

Throughout the pages of this book, you will learn to recognize what you've been given to manage and how to manage it to God's glory and honor. You will learn different ways to "go forth and be fruitful." Finally, you will learn what to do with the fruits of your labor to expand God's kingdom and his people. These three phases make up the Fiscal Stewardship Cycle.

Hang on tight. This is going to be a fun ride.

What Have I Been Given? What Is Stewardship?

Stewardship

The LORD God took the man and put him in the Garden of Eden to work it and take care of it.

Genesis 2:15 (NIV)

Then God blessed Noah and his sons, saying to them, "Be fruitful and increase in number and fill the earth.

Genesis 9:1 (NIV)

Joseph found favor in his eyes and became his attendant. Potiphar put him in charge of his household and he entrusted to his care everything he owned. From the time he put him in charge of his household and all that he owned, the LORD blessed the household of the Egyptian because of

> Joseph. The blessing of the LORD was on everything Potiphar had, both in the house and in the field. So he left in Joseph's care everything he had; with Joseph in charge, he did not concern himself with anything except the food he ate.
>
> Genesis 39:4–5 (NIV)

So What Is Stewardship?

In the New Testament Greek, Jesus uses the word *oikonomia* (oy-kon-om-ee'-ah), which is the management of a household or of household affairs, specifically, the management, oversight, or administration of another's property. He also used the words *oikonomos* (oy-kon-om'-os) & *epitrops* (ep-it'-rop-os), which are the actual stewards, managers, overseers or curators who were given charge over a household or lands.

The Old and New Testaments were written in different languages. Our examples of Adam, Noah, and Joseph all come from the old Hebrew writings, so let's take a look at some of the word choices the Hebrew writers used. In the account of Genesis 39, Joseph is referred to as *paqad* (paw-kad) which is a verb meaning to pay attention to, observe, or to attend to. The other word used to describe Joseph's role was as servant, or *sharath* (shaw-rath'), meaning to minister or to serve.

Equally, both the Old and New Testaments give credence to the idea of stewardship as an act of service towards another man's belongings. In the case of this text, we are examining the idea that God has given us responsibility over his creation and therefore his possessions.

It is important to note in each of the cases above that Adam, Noah, and Joseph were all given charge of something that was not their own. Rather, they were given the task of managing and caring for it.

I especially appreciate that God placed Adam in the garden "to work it and take care of it." If God gave this to Adam and expected him to work and care for what he had, how much more should we, with thousands of years of our forefathers working, care for what God has given us? We have example after example of how we should care for that which we've been given.

Unfortunately, we live in a society that suffers from entitlement. Entitlement is the attitude that we somehow deserve what we have or at least what we think we *should* have. Look at how hard our grand parents and parents struggled to make a living.

I recall in my teenage years hearing things like, "As long as you live in my house, you'll live by my rules," and, "When you earn the money, you can do what you want with it." Well, guess what? I did. I'm sure many of you did as well. Didn't we struggle to get out of our father's house so that we could make our own rules and get our own things?

I don't recall my father telling me, "Everything in my house is yours to do with as you please." Take a look at this Father: "'My son,' the father said, 'you are always with me, and everything I have is yours,'" (Luke 15:31, NIV).

What? I never had that one. Unfortunately, that is the message that God has been telling us all along. All we need to do is ask and it's ours. We fight and fight, thinking we have something to prove to the world. It's no wonder that we struggle with trusting God's provision. We've been fighting with the teaching of our earthly fathers.

My father tells me over and over again how he wishes he could have earned the living I enjoy now when he was trying to provide for us growing up. Many have multiple cars, televisions, gaming systems, DVD players, computers, etc. as well as the expectation of getting more. Yet the feeling that this is not enough plagues our society.

We live with hypersensationalism and hyperconsumerism at its best. We need things faster and more powerful—fast food, microwave popcorn, drive-thru pharmacies, online dating, online colleges, faster cars, , faster computers and internet speeds, and the list goes on about how we want things faster and faster.

We were shopping for Christmas presents this year when out of nowhere the elderly woman behind my wife started complaining about how slowly the line was moving. She was so impatient that she nearly pushed Belinda out of the way to save two minutes while she cut in line. The cashier explained that she needed to get back in line and wait her turn, which made her more furious.

What is our world coming to when we feel so entitled? Mine! Mine! Mine! It sounds like my four-year-old yelling at her older sister. We discipline our children, but who is here to discipline us when we get to this point?

Have you ever taken something away from your child only to hear them yell and scream about how the toy is theirs? The discipline that follows has the tone of, "Did you pay for this toy? No. I didn't think so. Your mother and I paid for it. It is ours. You need to recognize that we can take all of your toys away if you can't take care of them properly and share..." Yes, I'm sure you've had or heard these conversations. I've been guilty of this regularly.

Take a look back at Genesis in the garden. When Adam and Eve broke the one sacred rule of not eating from the tree of knowledge of good and evil, they lost their home in paradise. A curse was put on them and on the land in which we still live.

Stewardship. Hmm. This is a concept that has been around since the beginning of mankind. We did not make the earth or set out the boundaries of the water. We did not breathe life into man. God did all of this, and he expects us to work it and care for it, as it is all his.

Considering that we live in his world and everything we have comes from him, let's evaluate how we're doing. The primary focus of this book is fiscal stewardship; therefore, let's keep our eyes on financial matters. However, keep in mind that stewardship is more than just money management. It is also management of your household, marriage, parenting, time, knowledge, gifts, etc. Stewardship is encompassing many different aspects of our lives.

What Have I Been Given?

Provided in the back of this book is an assessment called "What I've Been Given." It is very important that you go through this exercise and assess the things you've been given; otherwise, you will not gain the right perspective with the rest of these materials. Every chapter from here on out will build on this idea. The lessons will be much more powerful when you do the work associated.

Go ahead and stop now to complete the exercise. When you complete it, go ahead with the rest of the reading.

Good. Now you're either thanking God for all you've been given or you're saying to yourself that you haven't been "given" any kind of special financial treatment. You've had to pull yourself up by your bootstraps and work hard for the things you have. I've heard all kinds of excuses. Do any of these sound familiar?

- Why do other people who make the same as me have all the luck?
- I didn't finish college; therefore, I'll never be successful.
- I didn't come from the right family.
- It's who you know, after all.
- The government just taxes it, so why try?
- The rich just keep getting richer, taking advantage of hardworking guys like me.
- Are you kidding? I've got more month than I do money.
- Money doesn't grow on trees.
- I'm not good enough.
- Blah, blah, blah.

Do you get envious of other people when it seems that things come very easily? I did when I was younger and still fight the temptation today. I was envious of people that were able to go to college on mommy and daddy's dime. I was envious and jealous of the new cars pulling into the parking lot at my high school. I was envious and jealous of kids with parents who were still married or of people living in houses rather than the apartments we lived in.

When I was a freshman in college (I haven't finished my degree yet, by the way) in 1994, I drove a 1989 Acura Integra. See, in high school, the Integra was the "rich" kid's cool car. When I started working, I wanted to be like them. Some of the other kids on campus used to yell out profanities at me as I drove by about being rich or getting it from "mommy or daddy." I would get angry and come back with some slant about working hard and paying for it myself. Unfortunately, I felt very proud of myself in those moments. Oh yeah. Look at me.

The only thing that any of the envy or jealousy got me was a lack of friends and a burning rage inside that I could not quench.

Today, I still wrestle with envy of people who have achieved a higher level of success. What helps me find perspective is going back to God and realizing that he gave me everything I need for life and godliness through knowledge of him (2 Peter 1:3, NIV). I also reflect on:

> But remember the LORD your God, for it is he who gives you the ability to produce wealth.
>
> Deuteronomy 8:18 (NIV)

Wait a minute! I need to repeat that one again with emphasis.

> But remember the LORD your God, for it is he who gives you the ability to produce wealth.
>
> Deuteronomy 8:18 (NIV)

Read this entire chapter to get the context. I'll come back to it more when we get to the asset section of our course. For now, let's not lose focus on what we've been given.

That passage rang so true to me a few years back. God gave us the ability to produce wealth. He wants us to have abundance, just not at the expense of forgetting him.

You see, I now realize—and my hope is that you will also realize—that whatever you want to achieve is within your God-given ability to do.

How cool is that? That means that there are no longer any excuses for not reaching out for your dreams. It also means that the creator of the universe is the giver of the universe.

Anyone who doesn't recognize what he's been given thinks he needs so much more to find happiness. Maybe a new outfit, new car, food, new relationship, or even a new job will provide what you're looking for. Think through this one again.

God has already provided everything any of us needs. He has also declared to us, "For I know the plans I have for you, plans to prosper you and not to harm you, plans to give you hope and a future," (Jeremiah 29:11, NIV). Belinda and I had this verse on our wedding invitations. I've got to remember this promise so many times when I start thinking that I should be doing so much more.

So, with this in mind, here are some of the many blessings that God has given me, which help keep things in perspective. Take some time to go back over your assessment.

My hope is to inspire you to think outside the box while doing your assessment. Just because I didn't have the question in the assessment doesn't mean you can't add it somewhere. It's your assessment of what God has given you. Take ownership and make it yours.

I grew up disliking books and hardly reading any. Now I read ten to fifteen books a year, and I'm writing this one for you. In terms of Fiscal Stewardship, I am extremely thankful for the following things God has given me. Take off the "I don't have enough" hat for a moment and consider the things for which you are thankful.

- the ability to produce wealth
- unfailing promises of prosperity if I seek him
- unfailing promises of hope and a future
- the ability to read and write
- my vision
- my dexterity to write
- the ability to reason and think clearly
- knowledge of him
- worldly training in financial matters
- books and ideas of people all over the world blessing me with their perspectives
- a warm bed in which to rest my eyes

- I own my fourth home (I never thought I'd buy one)
- health to be able to work
- freedom to do what I love to do
- communication skills
- many, many trials that teach me many of life's lessons
- other people's mistakes
- my own mistakes
- good credit (not always the case)
- cars to get me where I need to be
- relationships with people who introduce me to people who know more than me
- relationships with people with whom I can share my ideas
- mentoring relationships
- people I am able to teach (I retain more when I am teaching)
- passion for people's wellbeing
- integrity and character
- perseverance
- a supportive wife and family who want me to succeed in my dreams
- God wants me to succeed
- God made me, in his likeness, fierce
- God gave me his spirit to guide my steps

- God has given me many advisors to ensure success
- I've been given money with which I can use to bless others and provide for my family
- We've been given great health that keeps us going
- a vision of something much bigger than me
- a desire in my heart to fight the enemy
- shoes to protect my feet while walking to appointments
- computer literacy for research and marketing
- ideas and thoughts
- people who love me

I could go on; but you see, unless you have a clear idea of what God has given you to manage, your attitude won't align properly with the attitude that a steward of God's household should have.

Look at some of the characteristics of Joseph (found in Genesis 39).

- He found favor in his master's eyes (boss?)
- Everything he did prospered
- He was dedicated to the Lord, regardless of his circumstances
- He was trustworthy
- He had High standards of integrity
- He had leadership skills

- He was very healthy (well-built and handsome)
- He refused at his own expense to break the rules (sleep with Potiphar's wife)
- He honored his master and knew his place
- He knew that his sin was against God and Potiphar
- He did not defend himself when falsely accused

There are many qualities of a steward in God's household that Joseph depicts. The most important was his dedication to the Lord in all things before dedication to the things.

As we journey on this road together over the next several days and weeks, be sure to dedicate your financial affairs to the Lord in prayer. Think about how you use the money he's entrusted you with. Is it to honor him or you?

By trusting him, by surrendering all to him (it's his anyways), and by dedicating yourself to him, God will make everything you do prosperous, just as he did with Joseph.

I look forward to hearing about your success and your struggles in your journey to let go and let God. He has entrusted his household to you and trusts that you will manage it all well.

Again, if you haven't completed your personal assessment of what you've been given, please close this book and complete that worksheet before continuing to chapter 3.

Being Fruitful with What God Gave You

Go to the ant, you sluggard; consider its ways and be wise! It has no commander, no overseer or ruler, yet it stores its provisions in summer and gathers food at harvest. A little sleep a little slumber, a little folding of the hands to rest—and poverty will come on you like a bandit and scarcity like an armed man.

Proverbs 6:6–11 (NIV)

And God said to him, "I am God Almighty; be fruitful and increase in number. A nation and a community of nations will come from you, and kings will come from your body. The land I gave to Abraham and Isaac I also give to you, and I will five this land to your descendants after you."

Genesis 35:11–12 (NIV)

Now the Israelites settled in Egypt in the region of Goshen. They acquired property there and were fruitful and increased greatly in number.

Genesis 47:27 (NIV)

What Does It Mean to Be Fruitful?

We have already established that God placed Adam and Eve in the garden to work and take care of it. One of Adam's roles was to care for the orchard that ultimately spelled our doom.

How would you like that baggage and guilt hanging around your neck like an albatross?

Nonetheless, fruitfulness is simply starting something as a seed, a thought, an idea, a sum of money, a piece of knowledge, or salvation and growing to bless others with it.

Let us consider Webster's.

> Fruit: a plant, crop, or product. Or as a result or outcome <the fruit of labor>
>
> Fruitful: Producing fruit or producing abundantly

Let's take a look at the tree. After all, didn't Jesus destroy the fig tree that didn't produce fruit? Look at this example:

> Early in the morning, as He was on his way back to the city, He was hungry. Seeing a fig tree by the road, He went up to it but found nothing on it except leaves. Then He said to it, "May you never bear fruit again!" Immediately the tree withered.
>
> Matthew 21:18–19 (NIV)

Doesn't the tree produce the fruit for two purposes?

First, the fruit of the tree bears its seed to reproduce itself. Second, the fruit is food to bless the patron who dares to eat.

Who will care for the fruit-bearing tree? Someone must water, fertilize, feed, prune, and even graft in to bear fruit. Unfortunately, the work cannot always be done by oneself. Have you ever seen a plant or tree care for itself? Even in nature, trees are dependent upon water sources, birds, and bees to pollinate; the wind to scatter seeds; fires to thin out forests; etc.

If you've ever had a garden, you know that a garden requires constant care to grow. The plants do not bear good fruit if the gardener doesn't care for them. In order for the plants to grow good fruit, someone other than the plant must care for and nurture it.

In our own lives, God designed us to care for one another. When we are left to care for ourselves, the ugliest parts seem to take over. As a result, we rot from the inside out, producing poor fruit. In our lives, it is important to have relationships with others who tend to the weeds and rotten parts that come out in our fruit so that we can bear good fruit.

In our financial lives, the role of "gardener" is played by trusted advisors who have proven to honor God as well as having experience in the area of financial need you have. In order to be fruitful and abundant in your financial life, you must have a coach who helps you to create an easy to follow plan. Keep it simple.

Don't get me wrong. You can go at it alone, which is the proven method of most people. The only problem with that methodology is that the fruit and lack of abundance is less than desirable when considering most people.

If you want to fast track your abundant financial life, using a coach or mentor is a great way to grow and care for your harvest. Due to his or her experience, your coach or mentor will be able to help you grow when adversity strikes.

Consider 2008. Had God not provided many coaches and mentors for me to call on during our financial crisis, I'm not sure how I would have handled our situation. Emotionally; mentally; and in many cases, financially, my coaches and mentors stepped up to help stabilize my world.

My absolute biggest coach this last year was Jesus. The time I spent in prayer, study, and meditation, learning from Jesus has made all the difference. Without him, I'm confident that I would have snapped.

When looking for a coach or mentor, it is a good idea to find people who know more than you in the area with which you need help. Sometimes you'll be able to find them for free. Other times, you may need to pay a fee for their time. Either way, going at it alone will only produce rotten fruit. At best, you'll maintain what you currently have, perhaps a little more.

I like to think of abundance like a reservoir at the dam. The reservoir holds the water while the dam holds back the water until the abundance in the reservoir overflows the dam.

God's desire is to keep our reservoir so full that the dam can't hold back the flood.

> Bring the whole tithe into the storehouse, that there may be food in my house. "Test me in this" says the Lord Almighty, "and see if I will not throw open the floodgates of heaven and pour out so much blessing that you will not have room enough for it."
>
> Malachi 3:10 (NIV)

God wants us to recognize that his household is lacking food from the lack of abundance we have in our lives. He wants to pour out so much blessing that we won't be able to store it all. Where would we put it all?

Sadly enough, I found this true in my life. On the outside, our lives looked very abundant. Unfortunately, we made choices to finance our future. Let me explain. Our financial reservoir was empty many times; so rather than waiting for it to fill again, we used credit and created our own overflow. I see so many people out there who fall into the same trap.

The enemy, Satan, has lied to us. He is whispering that we won't have enough. He uses a line of thought like, *Did God really say he would pour out so much blessing that we won't have room for it? Did he really tell you he'll throw open the floodgates of heaven for you?*

Satan uses this cleverly designed tactic to make us question God. He doesn't lie to us directly, but he disguises his motives with questions to make us question. The *fruit* of his labor is that we live in a position of worry and *scarcity*.

For my family, that is exactly what 2008 looked like. I was worried, tired from lack of sleep, short with my temper, and scared of what the future would hold for us. The promises that I held on to were not from God. They were the promises of hunger, homelessness, and loneliness.

The opposite of *abundance* is *scarcity*. Scarcity can also be known as *bad fruit*. It paralyzes us and creates fear. To realize the true desire of God for our *fruitfulness* is to *believe wholly* in his promises and to leave the questioning to Satan.

It is time to open your eyes to these truths, and open your mind to these ancient ideas about money. The reality of it is that scarcity rules in most households. It does not matter the size of the paycheck or bank account. I've seen people who have nothing and earn very little with a more abundant lifestyle than those who make hundreds of thousands of dollars per year.

Living Abundantly

> He replied, "The knowledge of the secrets of the kingdom of heaven has been given to you, but not to them. Whoever has will be given more, and he will have an abundance."
>
> Matthew 13:11–12 (NIV)

> You crown the year with your bounty, and your carts overflow with abundance. The grasslands of the desert overflow; the hills are clothed with gladness. The meadows are covered with flocks and the valleys are mantled with grain; they shout for joy and sing.
>
> Psalm 65:11–13 (NIV)

We were born in abundance with all we ever needed. God provided food, shelter, clothing, companionship, and purpose. He still provides it. We are surrounded by his grace and mercy every day.

I'll never forget my senior year in high school. My mother faced bankruptcy in her financial life. It was a very challenging time for us. She kept telling me that God would provide for us. She didn't know how; but from behind her tears, I knew that she believed it.

If you're not sure about God's promise of abundance, think back to his promise to Abraham about his descendants being more numerous than the sands and the stars. Now think about traffic today and ask yourself if God fulfilled his promise of abundance and fruitfulness to Abraham.

Okay, so Abraham didn't see the promise fulfilled in his lifetime.

Fair enough.

Think about Job, who had great abundance only to lose it in what many call a silly "bet" between God and Satan (see Job chapters 1 and 2,). What happened later in Job's life? Let's look.

> After Job had prayed for his friends, the Lord made him prosperous again and gave him twice as much as he had before ... The Lord blessed the latter part of Job's life more than the first.
>
> Job 42:10–12a (NIV)

The reason Job gained back his inheritance plus more was the fact that when he lost it, he recognized it as coming from the Lord and never stopped praising God. He did go through a period of questioning; but at the end of the day, he praised God and trusted him. As a result, the Lord blessed him beyond all measure.

What about you? Do you maintain an abundant attitude during difficult times, or do you resort to scarcity?

Job did not worry about his homes, money, business, servants, and family being lost. He focused his energy on God and asked what he should do. Job was surrounded by scarcity; and believe it or not, you will be too. All of Job's friends and family wanted him to give up on his God and kill himself.

"Take matters into your own hands," they said.

Wow! Can you imagine? It's hard to believe that the people who "love" us most can be a cancer to us when we face financial challenges.

With an attitude of abundance, that is not possible. When we recognize what God has given us to manage for him, the amount doesn't matter. We only know to be fruitful with it.

Unfortunately, God didn't give us a set of instructions with step-by-step instructions for managing his household. The exciting thing is that God gave each of us the ability and creativity to produce great wealth without instructions.

Your self-limiting belief system is the only thing limiting your reservoir. Make some changes to the integrity of your dam, oh great dam engineer. God has not only given you permission; he promised it.

It is time to re-engineer your thoughts and beliefs about God's abundant promises for you. These promises are for you and your children and your grandchildren and for those who are far off. Decide and go for it.

Through abundance, thousands of hungry children around the world will eat today. Do you realize more children need you to live abundantly?

Through abundance, thousands were given homes after hurricane Katrina.

Through abundance, thousands will live due to disease research and cures.

Through abundance, thousands of unwanted daughters of China have American families.

Through abundance, the gospel message is spread over

every continent on the earth. When faced with certain death, faith abundantly persevered.

Through abundance, our church provided a family of eighteen kids with a Christmas they will never forget. Each child had three to four gifts and food to last several days.

Through abundance, someone shared the gospel message of Christ with you and me. Overflow happened.

Through abundance, you are able to read this book. The overflow of someone's ability to read came rushing into your life.

Only through abundance does the work of Christ prevail. Abundance is the work of the Spirit in your heart, prompting you to give a little more when you see a hungry child on the road.

Do you remember that it was from abundance that Jesus left to come rescue us on the cross? He traded wealth for extreme poverty. He traded life for death. He traded himself for you and me. He emptied himself of everything, but did he really lose anything?

Don't lose hope in the abundance of the Lord.

It is now your turn to live the abundant life God promises you. Your family needs you. Your neighbor needs you. Your country needs you.

Do we need another economic bailout or stimulus package? No. We simply need an attitude adjustment. We are such an abundantly wealthy nation. You are abundantly wealthy.

If you lack, it's simply the message you are telling yourself. Change the message, start overflowing into the lives of those around you, and see if God doesn't pour so much into your lap that you don't know what to do with it all but to give it back.

Scarcity

This one is tough.

Have you ever come to the end of the month with four or five days until you get paid again and have only a few dollars left in your account? You don't have any food, the car is out of gas, and the church is asking for your tithe. What do you do?

If you're like most, you will put a little gas in the car and eat. After all, the church is supposed to help those in need. You rationalize with yourself, "I'm in need. Therefore, this week's contribution is serving God by taking care of my needs."

Hmm. Put like that, it sounds a little selfish, doesn't it? Doesn't it sound self-sufficient, just a little self-reliant?

Before too long, the tithe takes a backseat to every other need you may have. I once saw a man struggling to find work. He was depressed due to his inability to "provide" for his family. He didn't have the money to tithe or to help anyone else for that matter.

It was interesting to see him with a forty-four or sixty-four-ounce fountain drink every time I saw him. I saw him a couple of times a week with a similar drink. A few times, he had fast food meals with him.

Have you ever done that? I have. It is so easy to make a decision not to do something beneficial for others or even for your very self yet spend money on empty calories and junk we don't need. The very worry of not having enough for shelter or food robs through wasteful spending.

His thoughts pointed him toward a path of self-destruction where the only fruit he bore was that of lies. Satan whispers, "Did God really say . . . ?"

Scarcity creates a world of illusion and stress.

Scarcity is the driving force behind worry.

> Therefore I tell you, do not worry about your life, what you will eat or drink; or about your body, what you will wear. Is not life more important than food, and the body more important than clothes? . . . And why do you worry about clothes? . . . For the pagans run after all these things, and your heavenly Father knows that you need them. But seek first his kingdom and his righteousness, and all these things will be given to you as well. Therefore do not worry about tomorrow, for tomorrow will worry about itself. Each day has enough trouble of its own.
>
> Matthew 6:25–34 (NIV)

Wow! How much time do you spend worrying about things like food and clothes? I can tell you that I've spent many hours, days, weeks, and years worrying about these things. I've even taken it to the point where worry carried over to what other people might think. Wow! Absolute vanity.

I've traded sensible financial management to "buy" someone's opinion. The sad thing is that the other person couldn't care less about what I'm doing. Scarcity of money leads to scarcity of social position. The idea goes something like this: "Somehow, if I show that I live in a way which appears poor, I will then lose friends or won't be accepted anymore."

Have you ever had thoughts like this? My friend, you're not alone. In a room of one hundred people, I'm sure that 99 percent of the room will raise their hands. The other one will be too embarrassed to raise his hand due to what people will think about him.

I hated growing up in apartments. My parents did the best that they could with what they had. I appreciate the work they did to provide for us, but I vowed that my family would own a home and have some security. Apartment living somehow was shameful. I wanted to fit in with the "rich" kids who lived in nice neighborhoods.

We have lived in nice homes since we've been married, but the homes haven't filled the void I felt when I was a child.

Unfortunately, my needy scarcity mindset pushed those people away anyways. Living to please others is a huge indicator of scarcity in your life.

Since God has blessed us with a home of our own, I've had plenty of worry about our home and food. I've spent hours crying with Belinda, explaining how I only want our girls to have more than I had growing up.

See, I have lived my life from a position of scarcity since childhood. There were times when my father was on strike and we were on food stamps. The cars were repossessed after a period of dramatic salary decrease. We went through bankruptcy while I was in high school. We never seemed to have enough. What does that mean exactly? Truth. I have always been healthy. I've never slept on the street. I've always had warm clothes. For the most part, I even eat every day. These are lessons of the manna. Give us this day our daily bread.

Scarcity is an *arrogant* attitude that says I deserve more and should be able to get what I want when I want it. It leads to entitlement thinking. This is a very sad and dangerous place from which many Christians to live their lives.

It has been hard for me to trust that God would provide more than enough. No. All I ever knew was scarcity. But now, I hold on tightly to the promises of Jeremiah 29:11 with a firm grip, knowing confidently that God has great plans for my family. What a great reminder and a great promise.

Belinda is the extreme opposite. She didn't come from an extremely wealthy family. But they always gave what they had, and there was always enough to get by thanks to God. They are very God-fearing and trusting that God always provides. She grew up in an abundance household.

God blessed me greatly the day he gave me Belinda. She is my gift from God to always remind me of his abundance and love in my life. She is my compass, always directing me back to God, who provides from his overflowing.

In scarcity, we avoid giving a tithe.

In scarcity, we make late payments on debts.

In scarcity, we fail to act on opportunities that can get us ahead.

In scarcity, we believe that we have too much to lose if we act.

In scarcity, we wish our starving friends good luck.

In scarcity, we rent because a house is too big of a commitment.

In scarcity, we don't save for the future because we

don't earn enough. (They say that alcohol, cigarettes, and chocolate are recession-proof.)

In scarcity, we believe that we are saving money when advertisers convince us to buy their gadgets.

Scarcity is the number one reason for worry, stress, heart disease, physical fatigue, depression, and many other physical ailments.

> Be self controlled and alert. Your enemy the devil prowls around like a roaring lion looking for someone to devour.
>
> 1 Peter 5:8 (NIV)

Scarcity is the devil in disguise waiting to devour. Be aware of these things.

Care for the Fruit

When considering how we are fruitful with what God has given us, it is important to keep our attitudes in check.

God's plan for fiscal stewardship dictates that we recognize what we've been given and then develop the fruit. Being fruitful is our attitude toward God's rich abundance in our lives and our ability to grow and develop what he gave us.

Remember the parable of the talents (Mathew 25:14–30, NIV)? In the parable, Jesus tells of three men who were each given talents. The two who grew their share were given more while the one who fearfully hid away his talent lost it.

The key is that they were not given instruction on what to do with what they had been given. They were entrusted what was according to their ability. Then the owner left for a journey.

Isn't it cool how God knows that we will muck things up, yet he entrusts so much to our care? Okay. Even cooler than that is that he doesn't tell us how to do it. He says, "Just do it." Go Nike.

So, what are you doing to develop what God gave you? I hope that you've completed the assessment of what God has given you.

Stop reading, and ask yourself how you are growing each of the areas or what you are doing with them. Record your thoughts on each.

Do you like to read? No? Sadly, studies have been done that show that greater than 70 percent of adults have not read a book since they graduated high school or college.

The common attitude about self-help workshops and conferences is that they are a waste of money. That is interesting. Listen to who makes those comments and consider if they have the sort of developed abundance you're seeking. I would venture to say no.

I work in the mortgage industry, which has multiple opportunities for trade conferences geared at educating the sales force in my industry. With over five hundred thousand mortgage loan officers in America, only two to three thousand show up for an annual event I attend. Now, to put that in perspective, three thousand people out of five hundred thousand is 0.6 percent of the people in our industry devoted to developing their skills. Now, this number is off a bit since there are multiple conferences.

It is probably closer to 1.5 percent who actually spend the money to grow and develop their fruit.

When we talk with the top producers in the industry, they credit their success to things they learned from conferences, books, audio programs, and other self-help vehicles. Any surprise here? I didn't think so. These top producers see abundance in their careers and lives because they seek to develop their talents.

These numbers are staggering when you consider that this is their livelihood. So many choose to be the third man in the parable of the talents yet don't even realize that this is how they live.

What are some of the ways they develop themselves? What are the names of the top twelve on *American Idol*? Do you remember the Soup Nazi on *Seinfeld*? Can you tell me about the house project on *Extreme Home Makeover*? Who got voted off of *Survivor*? Academy awards? Who is Jennifer dating now, or is she still heartbroken over Brad?

What will these trivial facts of others' success do for you? Have you ever seen an apple tree jealous of another apple tree, wishing its apples were bigger, redder, or shinier?

Many laugh about my expenditure in conferences and more learning. Today, many of my colleagues are looking for new work due to market conditions. Their lack of development bore bad fruit, which cannot support their careers.

After all, as God's loved and chosen child, I owe it to him to work for him and not for men (Colossians 3:23,).

Jesus was known as one who spoke with authority and grace. He was known for his excellent work ethic. If I truly believe that I am following him, I should strive to have a similar work ethic.

There are countless books out there covering every topic imaginable. It has been said that if you read for one hour a day on any topic, you will be an expert on that topic in two years.

Reading is one of the most cost-effective ways to develop your skills and knowledge in any area that you are looking to improve. God expects it.

When considering your financial health, he says with emphasis:

> I love those who love me and those who seek me find me. With me are riches and honor, enduring wealth and prosperity. My fruit is better than fine gold; what I yield surpasses choice silver. I walk in the way of righteousness, along the paths of justice, bestowing wealth on those who love me and making their treasuries full.
>
> Proverbs 8:17–21 (NIV)

Simply studying the book of Proverbs will give you all you need for life and godliness. There are thirty-one books in Proverbs. With thirty to thirty-one days in a month, you can read one chapter every day in a month and meditate on the meaning.

I recommend that anyone wanting to understand God's principles of fiscal stewardship must read Proverbs several times through to get a complete picture of God's promises of money management. I read Proverbs nearly every day. I've been camped out on a daily pursuit of these gems now for three years. Pick up several of the Bibles in our house and see if you can read past my notes in Proverbs. I change Bibles about every six months for the simple fact that new things pop out at me from the book, and my notes and different color highlights make it difficult to decipher after a little bit of my study.

To gain a better understanding of being fruitful with what God has given you, please go back and ask how you are developing the things God has given you from the assessment.

Development is simply watering God's fertile garden. He will make it grow.

> I planted the seed, Apollos watered it, but God made it grow. So neither he who plants nor he who waters is anything, but only God, who makes things grow. The man who plants and the man who waters have one purpose, and each will be rewarded according to his own labor. For we are God's fellow workers; you are God's field, God's building.
>
> 1 Corinthians 3:6–9 (NIV)

A Cheerful Giver: Blessing Others with Your Abundance

Go to the ant, you sluggard; consider its ways and be wise! It has no commander, no overseer or ruler, yet it stores its provisions in summer and gathers food at harvest. A little sleep a little slumber, a little folding of the hands to rest—and poverty will come on you like a bandit and scarcity like an armed man.

Proverbs 6:6–11 (NIV)

Remember this: whoever sows sparingly will also reap sparingly, and whoever sows generously will also reap generously. Each man should give what he has decided in his heart to give, not reluctantly or under compulsion, for God loves a cheerful giver... Now he who supplies seed to the sower and bread for food will also supply and increase your store of seed and will enlarge the harvest of your righteousness. You will be made rich in every way so that you can be generous on every occasion, and

> through us your generosity will result in thanksgiving to God
>
> 2 Corinthians 9:6–15 (NIV)

Okay, so we've looked at what it is that God has given us. And we've also discussed the attitude we should have about what he's given us in abundance. We know that we should develop the fruit to make it grow and multiply.

Now let's turn our thoughts and discussion to why all of this is important.

Let's revisit the parable of the talents (Matthew 25:14–30) as well as the parable of the ten minas in Luke 19:11–29 to get a clearer idea of what Jesus taught on the matter of what giving back looks like after receiving and developing.

First, let's take a look at *give* or *giving* as defined by Webster's Dictionary: 1. to make a present of (gave them money for their birthdays), 2. To put temporarily at the disposal of (gave us the beach house for a week).

There are quite a few other definitions in the dictionary for the word *give*, but these fit the purposes of fiscal stewardship best.

First of all, giving is a gift. We've already established that we were given a great gift and responsibility. We too must now take what we've developed and give it to someone else to bless their lives with no expectation of a return.

Second, the gift we received was given to us with the understanding that it was temporary and intended to be passed along. The cool thing about all of this is that the more you pass it along, the more you receive. It is much like a smile. The more you give, the more you receive.

When you give your gift, always give with the expectation that the recipient of your gift understands they must do the same for someone else later.

Like the Kevin Spacey movie, *Pay It Forward.* This giving is all about blessing the world. We've all heard of six degrees of separation. Imagine that, if we really are so connected, then with the more we give away, we can infect many others with this idea of giving in a relatively short period of time.

Get out there and give it away.

Let's get back to our parables of the talents and minas.

In each of the parables, two of the three men who received money took some sort of action to increase the owner's asset. Upon his return, he blessed them accordingly. Matthew describes it by saying that each man was put in charge of many things. Luke describes the similar parable that each man was given ten or five cities to oversee and manage.

Why did Jesus go to such elaborate lengths to describe these men? I believe that he was making a point about what to do with riches once you receive them.

These men had proven themselves in their ability to manage and increase that which was not their own. After doing so, they were put in charge of a greater area of responsibility to increase it. I believe that in order to increase their areas, they had to teach others their skill set in multiplying money.

It was now their responsibility to train others in their skills and arts. Now, in their abundance, it was time to give back the wisdom or the applied knowledge of their learning. It was now time to preach and teach what they first practiced.

Unfortunately, too many people try to preach and teach from a position of not having first practiced.

Look back at 2 Corinthians 9 when Paul is describing our role with our wealth. In our riches, we are to be generous. By the measure we sow, we will receive. Give away what you have and see if it doesn't come back to you ten times over.

It is absolutely amazing to me how God blesses our efforts. Let's take a few more looks at some other ways God wants us to use what he has given us.

> I tell you, use worldly wealth to gain friends for yourselves, so that when it is gone, you will be welcomed into eternal dwelling.
>
> Luke 16:9 (NIV)

> Wealth brings many friends, but a poor man's friend deserts him.
>
> Proverbs 19:4 (NIV)

> A good man leaves an inheritance for his children's children…
>
> Proverbs 13:22 (NIV)

> Moreover, when God gives a man wealth and possessions, and enables him to enjoy them, to accept his lot and be happy in his work–this is a gift from God. He seldom reflects on the days of his life, because God keeps him occupied with gladness of heart.
>
> Ecclesiastes 5:19–20 (NIV)

> God gives a man wealth, possessions and honor, so that he lacks nothing his heart desires, but God does

not enable him to enjoy them, and a stranger enjoys them instead. This is meaningless, a grievous evil.

Ecclesiastes 6:2 (NIV)

The sluggard's craving will be the death of him, because his hands refuse to work. All day long he craves for more, but the righteous give without sparing.

Proverbs 21:25–26 (NIV)

If your enemy is hungry, give him food to eat; if he is thirsty, give him water to drink.

Proverbs 25:21 (NIV)

Give to the one who asks you, and do not turn away from the one who wants to borrow from you.

Matthew 5:42 (NIV)

But when you give to the needy, do not let your left hand know what your right hand is doing, so that your giving may be in secret. Then your Father, who sees what is done in secret, will reward you.

Matthew 6:3–4 (NIV)

Freely you have received, freely give. Do not take along any gold or silver or copper in your belts; take no bag for the journey, or extra tunic, or sandals or a staff; for the worker is worth his keep.

Matthew 10:8–10 (NIV)

Jesus replied, "They do not need to go away. You give them something to eat."

Matthew 14:16 (NIV)

If you want to be perfect, go, sell all your possessions and give to the poor, and you will have treasure in heaven. Then come follow me.

Matthew 19:21 (NIV)

Then he said to them, "Give to Caesar what is Caesar's, and to God what is God's."

Matthew 22:21 (NIV)

The King will reply, "I tell you the truth, whatever you did for one of the least of these brothers of mine, you did for me."

Matthew 25:40 (NIV)

All the believers were together and had everything in common. Selling their possessions and goods, they gave to anyone as he had need.

Acts 2:44–45 (NIV)

Then Peter said, "Silver or gold I do not have, but what I have I give to you."

Acts 3:6 (NIV)

All the believers were one in heart and mind. No one claimed that any of his possessions was his own, but they shared everything they had ... There were no needy persons among them. For from time to time those who owned lands or houses sold them, brought the money from the sales and put it at the apostles feet, and it was distributed to anyone as he had need.

Acts 4:32–35 (NIV)

> Remembering the words the Lord Jesus himself said: "It is more blessed to give than to receive."
>
> Acts 20:35 (NIV)

> We have different gifts, according to the grace given us ... If it is contributing to the needs of others, let him give generously ...
>
> Romans 12:6–9 (NIV)

> I ask you to receive her in the Lord in a way worthy of the saints and to give her any help she may need from you ...
>
> Romans 16:2 (NIV)

> If I give all I possess to the poor and surrender my body to the flames, but have not love, I gain nothing.
>
> 1 Corinthians 13:3 (NIV)

> And here is my advice about what is best for you in this matter: Last year you were the first not only to give but also to have the desire to do so. Now finish the work, so that your eager willingness to do it may be matched by your completion of it, according to your means.
>
> 2 Corinthians 8:10–11 (NIV)

As you can see, there are quite a few passages that discuss the idea of taking what you have and blessing others with it.

I've heard it said in Christian fellowship that people are waiting on the Lord to do this or that for them. Wait a minute. Some even say they don't want to take the job that will pay more because more money is a worldly desire.

What? So how is it that when you cry out for help, you don't take it when it is offered?

Get a grip here, people. God is trying to provide for you so that you can bless others. Only through earning more money will you have an overflow to bless others.

If you don't want to be worldly with your wealth, the answer is not avoiding it. The answer is, "Don't be worldly with your wealth," whatever that means to you. For one man may have a great abundance and hoard it for himself, yet one with very little will give away even that which he cannot afford to give away. Worldliness is merely a product of the attitude you have toward wealth.

Change your attitude. Don't turn your nose up at God's promise of prosperity and wealth for those who love him. He is giving you this blessing because he trusts that you will do good blessing others with it. Your false humility does not earn you any extra points.

Think about it like this. There are literally millions of children who will go to bed hungry tonight. By refusing a higher-paying job, you are refusing to take control of a portion of the world's money supply that can be used to help these kids have a meal.

It is so important that the kingdom of God learns how to create more wealth. I shared earlier that one of my biggest fears is that my kids would know hunger. Guess what. I now understand that this is one of God's biggest challenges as well. See, everyone is his child. He hurts for his kids who are not eating every day.

We have a responsibility to earn more so that we can give it out as God would have us do.

Don't get me wrong. We have an enemy at work against us. Does Satan try to give us big salaries and a great many luxuries to lure us away from God? Oh, you better believe he does. That's why we must be aware and alert, not evasive.

Who better to provide for the needs of his people than his people? If you don't have the right attitude about your possessions, it won't make a difference if you have a little or a lot. Your attitude is always with you.

Would you rather see large sums of money in the hands of people you know are not using it to glorify God, or would you rather have a little ambition to make the money God wants to give you to bless his people and his household?

It is a difficult quandary. I know.

Personally, I have a goal to earn enough money to retire from my income-producing job so that I can spend my time in my youth blessing God's household with what he has taught me about who he is. It will take money for that to happen. It will take people like you reading my books, subscribing to my curriculum, and teaching these lessons.

I can work hard and produce a bountiful harvest, or I can ask the good Christians I know to support my family and me. Or I can create my own wealth and use their gifts to bless others. Don't you hear so many times that church members just spend money glorifying themselves? Why don't they serve the world with their money rather than buy that big building and things? Well, that is exactly what I want to do.

I want to earn my living honestly and without asking for someone's tithe to support me. My goal is to give back to those who need it most. You can do the same. It's as easy as learning how and having the right attitude toward fiscal stewardship.

Again, I believe that in order to truly bless the church, I must not be a financial burden to the church. You don't have to be either. In the meantime, I am working diligently to see this plan through. I won't hold back what he's given me today but will use the resources at hand to bless others with what I've been given.

I encourage you to get your heart and mind around this idea. Only through a communal financial effort and strong fiscal stewardship of God's household will the church truly grow and make a difference in the global economy in which we live.

Fiscal stewardship is such an important aspect of our lives. It is time that we take a stand against the devil's schemes and glorify God with what he has asked us to work and care for, increasing it and multiplying it to his glory and honor.

Look at the church's early years in Jerusalem. "All the believers were together and had everything in common. Selling their possessions and goods, they gave to anyone as he had need," (Acts 2:44, NIV).

Remember that the three key principals to fiscal stewardship are:

1. Knowing what you've been given
2. Being fruitful—developing what you've been given
3. Being a cheerful giver: blessing others from the abundance of what you've been given

We've taken the time to lay the foundation for God's idea of fiscal stewardship from the scriptures. Next, we're going to shift into the more practical application of fiscal stewardship and start learning skills in the following areas:

- asset management
- liability management
- lifestyle management
- renting versus buying
- passing on legacy

As we go through this next section, my goal is for you to gain some basic skills, knowledge, and ideas on how to improve your personal financial health so that you can put God's principles into practice.

My prayer is that God's hand will work powerfully, changing you from a consumer to conserver and from a conserver to a very cheerful and generous giver.

America has become a fast food, microwave oven, instant popcorn culture with a strong entitlement stronghold.

If you live a life with multiple credit cards, car payments, furniture payments, etc., and don't know how you managed to rack up all of your debt, it is because you've bought in to the lie that is the American entitlement dream. Trust me. I've been there. I'm a recovering entitlement junkie.

Overextending our debt because we qualify to do so is not a strong enough reason to mismanage God's household so that we can live a lifestyle we can't afford to live. Again, I did not believe I was doing this until my income source went away. Boy, did I find out quickly how overextended we were living.

Our lifestyle and practices were challenged in 2008. We thought that we were doing well, putting money in savings every month and paying our bills on time. We quickly found out that our savings weren't enough and our credit obligations were more than enough.

Practicing patience goes a long way in preserving health, relationships, and a cheerful attitude of giving generously.

It's time to take back control of your financial life from the grips of the enemy so that you can be a blessing to your neighbors and glorify God in the process.

This is not going to be easy. Be prepared to face challenges that are very emotional and have a stronghold in your life. I can assure you that as we go through these steps, there is not a quick solution to the situation you are in. You didn't arrive here overnight, and you won't get out of this position overnight.

It will take work on your part. It will require you to be honest with yourself; your spouse; and your closest friend, who will need to help you.

It is also going to require you to make lifestyle and habitual changes in the way you manage your finances through the choices you make daily.

I do promise you. If you will take the challenges placed before you and put these things into practice, the following things will enter into your life:

- a greater sense of peace
- stronger, more faithful relationships

- debt-free living
- increased savings
- stronger credit scores
- a closer relationship with God

I also promise that if you are not wholehearted in your efforts, your results will not reflect positive change. More than likely, you will find yourself more frustrated than you are today. We're riding a thin line. It will hurt to make the necessary changes to work toward success.

It has been said by many over the years, "If you want different results, you have to practice different habits. Insanity is defined as doing the same things over and over, expecting different results." You don't have to be like this. The cool thing is that God made you and gave you the ability to produce wealth. You can do this. God said that you can and made you to do so.

In order to break free from the bondage of the enemy, tough decisions will need to be made. Know that I am with you in this journey.

There are no excuses. There will be a lot of opportunity to make excuses, but none will be tolerated. To make radical changes in your life, radical steps need to occur. Your decisions need to be radically different than yesterday, or no change will occur.

Hang on. This is going to be fun.

What Is an Asset?

Go to the ant, you sluggard; consider its ways and be wise! It has no commander, no overseer or ruler, yet it stores its provisions in summer and gathers food at harvest. A little sleep a little slumber, a little folding of the hands to rest–and poverty will come on you like a bandit and scarcity like an armed man.

Proverbs 6:6–11 (NIV)

If you are wise, you are wise for your own benefit; if you are a mocker, you alone will bear the consequences.

Proverbs 9:12 (HCSB)

Lazy hands make a man poor, but diligent hands bring great wealth. He who gathers crops in summer is a wise son, but he who sleeps during harvest is a disgraceful son.

Proverbs 10:4–5 (NIV)

The house of the righteous has great wealth, but trouble accompanies the income of the wicked.

Proverbs15:6 (HCSB)

Now that we've gained an understanding of the Fiscal Stewardship Cycle in the context of God's financial blueprint, it is time to move forward in gaining fiscal literacy to strengthen our financial position. Only when we have a stronger understanding of the economy of money in our system will we be able to be true fiscal stewards in God's household.

There are three areas of fiscal literacy that are important to understand. All three of these areas interact and affect the others. Together, we call these the fiscal stewardship prosperity rings. The three rings are assets, liabilities, and lifestyle.

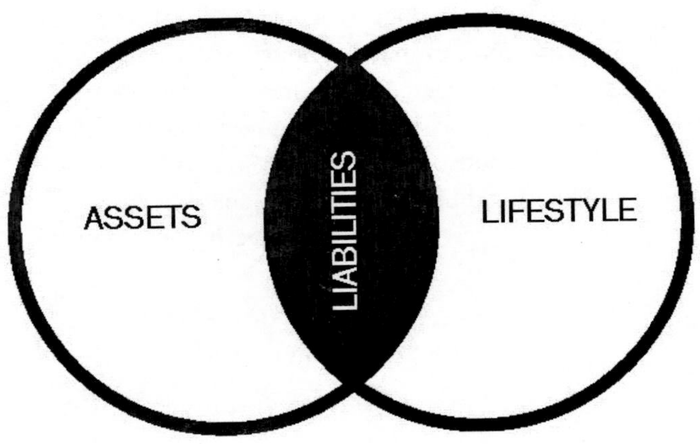

In this first section, we'll define an asset. With this knowledge, we'll understand some practical understanding of how wealth and prosperity come to be.

All three of these areas are important. Ultimately, it is in the category of assets where wealth and prosperity are measured.

As we look at assets, two areas are critical to develop if you don't already have them in place.

1. *Cash reserves*: 3 three to six months of gross income (before tax) in a liquid, easy to access account. This account is important to cover unexpected disruption to income or unexpected expenses that come up like a broken car, water heater, or distant funeral travel. Life comes at you fast, and things happen. If you don't have a reserve account, you will rely on credit cards, which can quickly zap your wealth.
2. *Savings plan*: How do you intend to afford retirement or college funding for your children? What about elderly care for loved ones? Funeral expenses? Travel to places you want to go to? A new car? A new home? A new business opportunity? You've got to have a plan to "gather food in the harvest and in season" so you will have enough to get through the off seasons in life.

What is an Asset?

Traditional financial planning and handbooks define an asset as an item that can be sold for cash value or cash itself. Assets are items that have market value.

The dictionary definition of an *asset* is: 1. A valuable material possession or 2. the entries on a balance sheet showing all properties and claims against others that may be directly or indirectly applied to cover liabilities.

What? Good night! No wonder people are afraid to make any financial moves. Our definitions are somewhat vague. Let's simplify this a little in terms that make sense.

Robert Kiyosaki, bestselling author (*Rich Dad Poor*

Dad), investor, entrepreneur, and educator, says, "Rich people acquire assets. The poor and middle class acquire liabilities, but they think they are assets."

Okay. So what is an asset according to Kiyosaki?

It's not the words that define an asset. The true definition of an asset or liability is in the numbers. What is the story in the numbers? When you look at your financial spreadsheet and see all of your assets, what do the numbers tell you?

This is a very important piece that you need to get. If you don't get this, this book and course will be a waste of your time. In order to grow your assets and increase your wealth and prosperity, it is essential that you can read the numbers and comprehend the story behind them.

Assets and liabilities have a "cash flow" pattern that is very simple to understand. Let's take a look to see if you can read and understand what is happening with an asset.

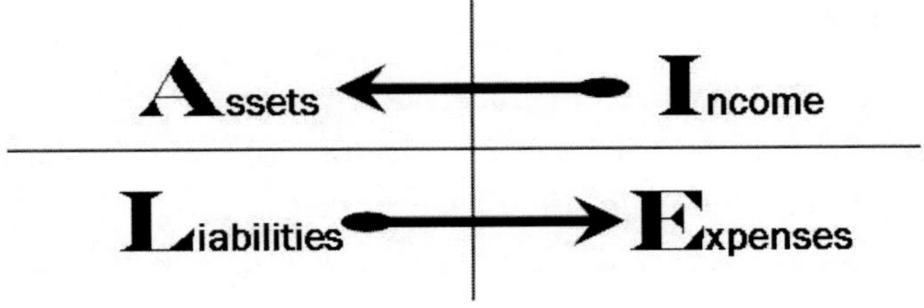

Do you see it? Is it very clear by looking at this picture?

Okay. Look at it again to see if you can figure out what an asset is for real.

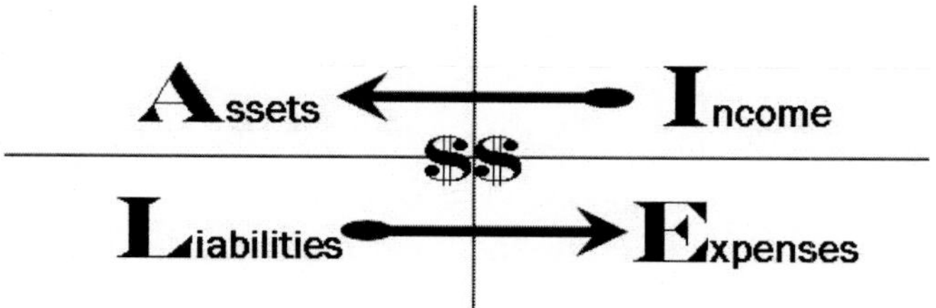

Okay. Now do you see it?

That's right! Assets create income. Mastering the prosperity quadrant is a critical component in understanding fiscal literacy that will transform your fiscal stewardship and take your financial life to new levels.

Before we can look at different types of assets, you've got to understand this concept clearly. So let's look at two of the most common mistakes people make when they look at their assets.

You own a car. You've visited www.kbb.com (Kelley Blue Book) to find the fair market value of your car. I'll use my 2000 Suburban as an example. It is the LT model, so all decked out with leather; factory wheels; third-row seats; two-wheel drive; factory mags; CD and DVD system; 135,000 miles; $9,610; is in good condition.

Great. So is this an asset or a liability? Don't answer yet. Let's look a little deeper at this scenario.

I bought the car in 2004 for $19,000. Has it held its value? Somewhat, but after four years of use, it is worth half the value. I've added seventy thousand or so miles to the car in that time, which required maintenance every three thousand miles or twenty-three times. My checkups cost on average $45 X 23 = $1,035. Don't forget the $750 I've spent on new tires since the purchase. I've also had to change my spark plugs and air filters a few times, totaling another $250 or so. Then there is the $1,300 I spent this year on a new ABS system for my brakes.

Okay. Let's total up the costs on this vehicle since ownership: $3,335 over four years or 1,460 days. This car has cost me $2.28 per day since I purchased it. But wait. I didn't add in the interest on the loan or the insurance I've had to carry on it since purchase. We also haven't counted the depreciation of $9,000 since purchase.

So, now do you consider this an asset or liability? Think back to the cash flow model above.

That's right. The car is a liability 100 percent and then some, but why do financial plans put the car in the asset column? Remember how they define an asset? Anything that has a fair market value. The car can be sold today for a fair market value of around $9,600 if someone is willing to pay it.

Okay. Let's look at another one that is a little more difficult.

Look at your home if you own it. Let's assume you purchased the home for $150,000 three years ago. Today, a fair market value for your home is $190,000. The market was good for a few years, giving you a $40,000 gain in your home's value. Pretty good, right?

And don't forget that each year, you've been able to use the interest on the house payments to save you over $7,500 in federal and state income taxes. After all, the tax deductibility of interest on a mortgage is one of the greatest advantages to owning a home.

Asset or liability? It's okay to look back at the cash flow diagram above.

Is your house creating income or is it an expense? Think about it another way.

If you lose your job today and have no income, will your home require money from you or will it provide money for you while you're looking for a new job?

Now you're getting it. Your home, although a great investment when compared to renting and throwing money away, is a liability until you sell it to cash in on gains.

So hopefully by now you have a more clear idea of what an asset is.

Let's move forward a bit to see some good examples of assets that can grow your wealth.

Earning Interest

Let's take a moment to understand interest. You either pay interest or earn interest. The goal of an asset is to earn you income without a lot of effort from you.

Albert Einstein was said to have defined compound interest as "the eighth wonder of the world."

I've also heard it said that the man who understands the power of compound interest will earn it. The man who does not understand the power of compound interest will pay it.

Decide for yourself which you'd rather do with interest—earn or pay. Since we're talking about assets, let's focus on the earning of interest.

To understand the power of compound interest, let's look at the *rule of seventy-two*, which is a mathematical formula to find out how long it will take your investment to double in value.

Divide 72 by the interest rate you are earning to find out how long it will take to double your investment. Let's say you have $10,000 earning 6 percent interest rate. 72/6 = 12, so it will take twelve years to double your original $10,000 to $20,000.

What if you can get an 8 percent return on your investment? That cuts the doubling time down to nine years. What about 10 percent? Yup. You got it. Now you're down to 7.2 years to double your investment.

Why is this important? When looking at your assets, your biggest ally is time. So let's look at the time value of money.

Rule of 72

Age 25	$ 5,000.00	6% (12 Yr)	Age 25	$ 5,000.00	10% (7.2 Yr)
37	$ 10,000.00		32	$ 10,000.00	
49	$ 20,000.00		39	$ 20,000.00	
61	$ 40,000.00		46	$ 40,000.00	
73	$ 80,000.00		53	$ 80,000.00	
			60	$ 160,000.00	
			67	$ 320,000.00	
			74	$ 640,000.00	

Do you see how understanding the time value of compounded interest is important to the future value of your asset?

At 6 percent, if you start at age twenty-five, your $5,000 only doubles four times by age seventy-three. But over the same period of time at 10 percent return, your money doubles seven times for a $560,000 difference.

Wow! When you're looking at investing, this is powerful.

What if you wait until you're in your thirties to invest

or save? Just change the ages up above and follow your life to whatever age.

By understanding this simple calculation with the rule of seventy-two, you can judge if your investment will help you reach your goal as quickly as you would like.

Banks and Their Role

Banks are interesting. I worked in retail banking with the largest bank in the United States for six years to start my financial career. Just before leaving, I managed a branch with eighteen employees and over $35,000,000 in deposits.

It was my responsibility to monitor our deposits, the cost of money, and our fee income to make sure my branch was profitable for the bank as a whole. We had very aggressive sales goals to meet.

What? Did I just say sales goals in the bank? That's right, sales goals. I thought banks were about service when I started the job. Boy did I learn that banks are not a service industry.

You may be asking what I was selling. You're probably thinking banks are a service provided to patrons for depositing their money. I can tell you that banks are one of the primary reasons you haven't acquired the wealth you should.

Because our schools and families don't provide a lot of financial training in life, most of us get our training from what the bank tells us is smart money management. We fall into believing that a positive balance in our checkbook at the end of the month is smart money management. Oh, and don't forget the accounts that round up to the next nearest dollar to transfer the "change" on purchases so you are "saving" money. Smart move.

Well, my friends, open your wallet and see whose name is on your credit card, mortgage, or car loan.

The banks make billions of dollars by borrowing from us at low rates (CDs, savings accounts, interest-bearing checking accounts, etc.) and lending back to us on auto loans, personal loans, home equity loans, credit cards, etc. at much higher rates.

Let's say you earn 4 percent on a CD. Then you borrow from the bank at 10 percent on average between all the different loans you have with them. The bank is now earning a 6 percent spread. They are making off with billions in profits from educating you on smart money management skills.

The banks understand the idea of assets and liabilities. They know that your liability is their asset. You pay an expense to them, and they receive income from you. It's all about the direction of the cash flow.

Your strategy? Can you turn the tides on the banks? Sure you can, if you know how.

Borrow from them at the lowest rates possible, and earn a higher return on your investments. It is a simple plan. We will talk more about this under the liability section of the book.

Paper Investments

This is known as playing the stock market. In the market, there are many things to understand to become a savvy investor. The markets represent a higher risk than other types of investments but are one of the easier investment vehicles to get into.

Stocks are investments in which you own a number of shares of ownership in the issuing company. They are also referred to as equities. Stocks are the hot and sexy investments. They represent higher risk along with higher potential for earnings. Stocks tend to be more exciting. When they are good, they are good. You will want to have a professional stockbroker or financial planner help you pick good stocks. Trading stocks is not for the lighthearted.

Mutual funds are a pool of professionally managed stocks that usually consist of anywhere from a few stocks to several thousand. The idea is to diversify your investment choice to mitigate risk. Mutual funds represent a good potential for earnings for the investor who doesn't have the time or the financial know how to pick individual stocks. They are also ideal for the investor, who wants to buy a more stable investment vehicle without having to actively manage the investment themselves.

Bonds are loans to companies. Municipalities (cities and states) typically sell bonds to raise money for various projects for schools or hospitals. The most common bond is the government EE savings bond. Corporations can issue bonds to raise money for projects. Bonds represent less risk as well as smaller returns. Because these are loans, they are typically more secure since the issuer is required to pay back the bonds to the investor.

Diversification is many times referred to as asset allocation. The idea is to spread out the different types of investments in your portfolio to limit the amount of risk according to your tolerance. This is a strategy many investors use to protect against the ups and downs of the market. This is very important if you have a one-time lump sum purchase.

Dollar cost averaging is a strategy that is important to understand if you have consistent investments on a monthly basis of smaller fixed amounts. Let's use $150 as your fixed amount. Due to market volatility, stock or bond prices vary each month when you make your purchase.

Dollar Cost Average

		Cost for 10 Shares				
January	$10 / share		15 shares	$100		
February	$15 / share		10 shares	$150		
March	$20 / share		7.5 shares	$200		
April	$10 / share		15 shares	$100		
May	$15 / share		10 shares	$150		
June	$10 / share		15 shares	$100		
July	$5 / share		30 shares	$50		
August	$7.5 / share		20 shares	$75		
September	$10 / share		15 shares	$100		
October	$20 / share		7.5 shares	$200		
November	$30 / share		5 shares	$300		
December	$20 / share		7.5 shares	$200		
Total	(avg.)	$14.37 per share	13 shares per month			
Total Invested		$1,800		156 shares	$1825 (120 shares)	

If you were to buy ten shares per month, it would have cost you $25 more and you would have thirty-six less shares.

Dollar cost averaging is the slow and steady way most millionaires work to retirement comfortably. They didn't worry so much about the market swings because they knew that their strategy would come out ahead. If you have a 401k, this is also the strategy you employ on a monthly basis but don't realize it.

Getting into the stock market is not so scary if you

have a good strategy going in. It can be incredibly risky if you are trying to mix multiple strategies. There are so many different ways to invest in the market. It is important for you to take the time to study and know your strategy or hire a highly recommended advisor who can guide you in this adventure.

Real Estate

Investing in real estate is a great way to increase your wealth and prosperity. The banks love to lend money on real estate investment because they know the limited risk that real estate has. Over time, appreciation averages near 5 percent. That doesn't sound very exciting, but remember the power of leverage.

Banks will allow as little as a 10 to 20 percent investment from you while they match 80 to 90 percent. The power of real estate investing is the low cost to get in. Remember that the 5 percent appreciation is on the full 100 percent of the property value, not your initial investment, and the bank doesn't want any of that back. So your 10 to 20 percent investment can yield very high returns over time.

In fact, the larger the investment you make, your return will decrease. Let me explain.

Take a purchase price of $200,000. Your minimum 10 percent investment is $20,000. In five years, the house appreciates to $225,000. Your gain is $25,000. Your initial $20,000 investment grew to $45,000 total equity or 225 percent of the original investment!

Now let's put a 20 percent investment of $40,000.

Same scenario, same $25,000 gain. Now your return is reduced to 62.5 percent. By putting more money into the investment, your efficiency rating has decreased.

Now keep in mind that owning real estate has many other factors to consider. Putting 20 percent down will improve your cash flow on a rental property. Your loan payments will be less, and there will be no private mortgage insurance cost. So even though the appreciation may not yield the return you're looking for, you may come out ahead based on the other factors.

Investing in real estate can potentially create passive rental income. You have a loan, but the renter is paying the mortgage while you get the benefit of any amount of rent greater than the mortgage payment, special tax deductions on investment real estate, as well as the appreciated value of the property.

Rental property can potentially create a great amount of wealth if properly leveraged using other people's money. That is a powerful thing to understand when purchasing any type of asset.

Anytime you can use someone else's money to fund your investments, you have a higher chance of increasing your wealth.

Some downsides to owning real estate as an investment include maintenance, vacancy, damages, and lack of liquidity.

We've already discussed the upsides.

Real estate can be a great vehicle to invest for retirement, college funding for kids, or to help the community in underserved areas.

Because real estate is the biggest economic stimulus to any region, you're investing in the local economy. Providing housing for people who are not in a position to own serves an essential need of shelter.

Business Opportunities

Owning a business is risky stuff. You have got to do your homework before jumping into new business adventures. But if you want to consider where true wealth and prosperity lie, then investing in business offers great reward opportunities.

The wealthiest people in America are invested in multiple businesses. In 2000, the top 1 percent of Americans owned over 40 percent of the country's assets and wealth. Is it your goal to join the wealthiest Americans in wealth creation? If your answer is yes, the area of business ownership may be an area you will want to pursue more with caution.

There are so many different types of business opportunities to look at, but the idea with growing assets is to create cash flow that is not dependent upon you to trade your time.

Before jumping in to any sort of business opportunity, seek a lot of advice. With many advisors, your plans succeed.

Historically, owning a business meant thousands of dollars in start up costs. Ray Crock did an amazing thing by showcasing the phenomenon of franchising with McDonald's. Today, there are hundreds and thousands of franchise opportunities available to the individuals who want to take the risk.

Interestingly enough, just to open conversation with McDonald's about the possibility of franchising, the interested party must have $250,000 of non-borrowed personal resources available. That is just to show you're a serious candidate for one of their franchises.

Most franchises follow a similar method. They require liquid capital anywhere from $50,000 to $250,000. Then they have their total investment that can run $25,000 on up to several Million depending on the name. The risk is great, but a successful franchise can also present a very nice return for the person who wants to take the risk.

Since the internet came to life in the mid-1990s, another business phenomenon called home based business has taken America by storm. Many home based business opportunities create affordability with low operating overhead for the business owners.

Home base businesses have become very attractive to people who want to clock out for the last time but don't have the capital to start their own traditional business. The upfront investment is typically a fraction of the traditional business model which provides the new business owner with the opportunity to get into a profit mode in a much shorter time frame.

Another popular business model to consider is multi-level network marketing (MLM). These companies usually have a great product offering that they want to get to the market, but they don't have the sales force to promote the product. Some big names you may recognize are Avon, Amway, Tupperware, and Mary Kay. All of these companies have great products that they spend thousands of dollars to develop. In order to take them to market, they need independent distributors to sell the products.

Most of these companies grow in two ways. First,

the distributors do a fantastic job of selling the products. Second, the distributors are rewarded with higher pay grades and incentives when they recruit new distributors. It is a very simple system and has proven to be very effective.

The challenge with MLM companies is the method in which the business opportunities are presented. Unfortunately, many independent distributors lack business training and therefore promote the money making aspect. As a result of pushing the money side of the business, many people joined these organizations with the wrong expectations and in turn labeled them as "Get Rich Quick" schemes.

I believe in the MLM business model for a couple of reasons. First, the upfront cost to start your own business distribution is usually less than $1,000, and in many cases, less than $500. Because the startup cost is low, the business owner can become profitable in a shorter time line.

Second, when done right, most MLM companies offer residual based income or passive income from the work of the distributors the business owner recruits. The more people the business owner helps to reach their goals, the better off he becomes. This type of business model can free up a person's time to serve those less fortunate than themselves as is fitting to the Lord.

As you can see, there are many different business models to choose from. If you are serious about owning a business, I can't stress enough how important it is to seek a lot of advice from people who are already successful doing what you want to do. Advice from your mom, dad, or uncle Billy may be great if they are doing what you want to do. If they aren't business owners, perhaps the advice they give will be jaded a bit. Be careful.

Finally, with any business you start, know that they all require work. They don't happen over night, but only those with the mental fortitude are successful. May God bless you in your desires.

Intellectual Property

This is an interesting type of asset. A few years ago, popular singer and song writer Michael Jackson got into some legal trouble. The asset he used to collateralize his legal fees were the rights to all of the Beatles music, which are worth millions.

Intellectual property are things like books, music, systems, software, etc. that create royalty income. You have to create the piece once, but it can be duplicated and sold over and over for profit.

This is a beautiful type of asset to own if it produces income for you. This is how many actors and songwriters make their living long after they've stopped working. Consider Elvis's estate. Although Elvis died in 1978, thirty years ago, his estate is still producing income and providing for his daughter and many other beneficiaries.

This is one of the more difficult assets to create because it needs to fill some void in another person's life, causing a purchase. If no one will buy it, it is just something that you put a lot of effort in to.

This type of asset also holds emotional value because of the creator's vulnerability put into creation. There is much more at stake with this type of asset.

Closing

Understanding assets is so critical to any financial success. Take the time to review your cash reserves and your savings plan for retirement or educational funding for your children.

Before you start an elaborate savings plan, make sure you have a cash reserve set up for emergencies. Once you start investing, you don't want to have to access for small emergencies. Keep your longer term investments as long-term investments, planning out ten years or more to be most effective.

In fact, the Wall Street Journal has been conducting a study of investments, looking at their average annual return in the stock market. Their study reveals the average annual return, looking at fifteen-year periods. Investors who did not make any changes to their original investment over fifteen years averaged 10.5 percent while investors who tried to time the market and missed the best thirty trading days over the same fifteen years only earned an average of 2.2 percent. An investor who missed the best sixty trading days due to their market timing ability reduced their return to a -3.2 percent annual return. Ouch!

The point is, any investing is meant to be slow and over time, as the ant would do. Come up with a strategy, execute your plan, and then stick to it. Don't allow your emotions to derail your entire long-term plan. Our ant friend is slow, steady, and patient in his asset investment strategies.

As we transition out of assets, we'll move into liabilities. Keep in mind that the way in which you manage your liabilities will directly affect what you can do to invest in assets. If you manage your liabilities poorly, chances are you will not have much in terms of assets.

The choices you make here have a lasting effect on you, your spouse, your children, and your community. You cannot call yourself a steward of God's household and mismanage what he's given you.

If you don't have cash-flow-producing assets working for you to create abundant living, you will have liabilities sucking the life out of you. This is Satan's plan.

It's interesting to consider when we are actually a slave to money. Jesus was clear that we can't serve two masters, God and money. When we don't have assets and choose credit cards to live our lives or car loans or any other type of credit to get what we want and need in life, money can become our master very quickly.

Let me explain this more clearly. What constitutes a slave? Anyone who is ruled over by another is a slave in the loosest sense. Using the assumptions above about credit cards, car loans, and other types of credit, let's look at what can happen over time of serving those obligations.

First, we might find ourselves in a great financial position. We sign up for the car loan with the $400 car payment and $20,000 balance over five years. We might even say, "No Problem, I can swing that payment." We justify that our old car is pushing 100,000 miles and may not be reliable any more. It's time to trade in for the new one even though there is nothing wrong with the old one. We are now legally bound to the creditor for the next five years or less if we can pay it off early. By that time, we might decide to trade in for a new one and take on a new five year note.

Second, we arrive at work one morning to find out the fortune 500 company, where you've given fifteen years of your life, is laying off 1,500 people. You panic hoping you'll make it through, but sure enough there is a pink slip in your box. Immediately, worry takes over with thoughts like, "How will we pay the mortgage, the car, the credit cards, the student loans, etc.?" or "How will I put food on the table?" or "Can I find another job earning the same wage?"

Third, we might start out optimistic with conversations at home about how much money is in savings to support the family through the rough time. We might even consider a lesser position to help for a short period while looking for new work.

Fourth, we start to slide into depression when the job interviews don't go so well. It's been six months, the unemployment benefit is out of time, and the kids need to see the doctor. With no job on the horizon and the savings dwindling, we start to juggle credit cards to buy groceries or pay other bills. When I was in this situation with my family, I was certain things would turn around! Arguments about money and survival become more common than they've ever been.

The worst part about living this scenario for over two years, with my family, was seeing others in need and not being able to help. I grew bitter towards my church family thinking they should know we need help. Every time another family received help, I grew more and more bitter. I slipped, as do many, into serving the wrong master in my house.

I will tell you from my own personal experience, the idol of money is a crafty little god in deed. He will sneak up on you when you least expect. You'll be in church or even praying about not worrying about the bills. He'll even let you keep up your routines of bible study and worship services. Worry is his trademark. He even lets us dismiss worry as something we all do and as part of life.

In time, many families fall to financial ruin. I've witnessed many men hanging their heads in shame for not being the provider and rock their families need. I've hung my own head in shame in bankruptcy court and while losing my home. We put on the mask and head off to the office or to church and pretend everything is ok, but I've known men who are too ashamed to tell their ministers, their friends, or even their wives for fear of losing her.

Marriages end every day as a result of the subtle attacks of the god of money and worry in our lives. Be careful with this one my friends. He's crafty. If you're not careful, you may not even know he is living with you as you read this very book. The earlier you can recognize him, the sooner you can get back to serving the one true God and following Jesus the Lord of Peace.

Creating abundance through proper asset growth actually frees you from the slavery of debt and being a slave to the lenders. Month after month, so many Americans work so hard earning a living only to sign over their checks to their masters at the credit card and loan companies out there.

With a little work to change your habits, breaking free can be a very exhilarating part of your life's adventure.

Go forth and prosper. Don't forget the ant, my friends. He is very small, yet he is very wise.

What Is a Liability?

> Go to the ant, you sluggard; consider its ways and be wise! It has no commander, no overseer or ruler, yet it stores its provisions in summer and gathers food at harvest. A little sleep a little slumber, a little folding of the hands to rest—and poverty will come on you like a bandit and scarcity like an armed man.
>
> Proverbs 6:6–11 (NIV)

> Do not conform any longer to the pattern of this world, but be transformed by the renewing of your mind. Then you will be able to test and approve what God's will is—his good, pleasing, and perfect will.
>
> Romans 12:2 (NIV)

Do you remember the drawing we learned about in the last section, assets? Look at the relationship between the assets and the liabilities. Now look at the relationship between lifestyle and liabilities.

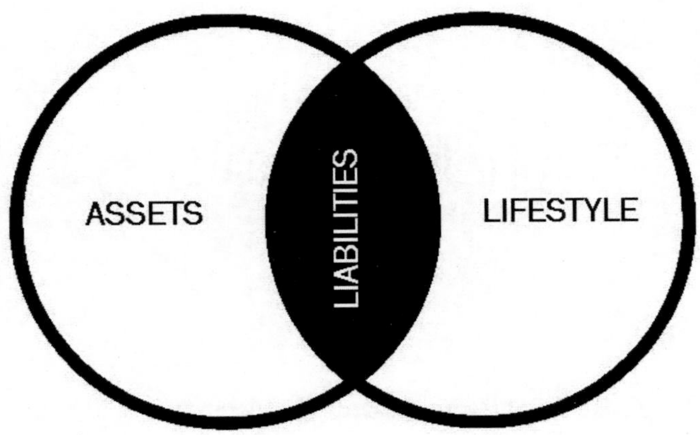

The fiscal stewardship prosperity rings show us that liabilities can make or break both assets and lifestyle if not managed well, so hold on as we go through this section. Have you ever heard anyone say, "I've got more assets than I know what to do with"? Or how about, "I'm in cash up to my eyeballs. Can anyone help me?"

No. I haven't heard any reference to having too much cash on hand.

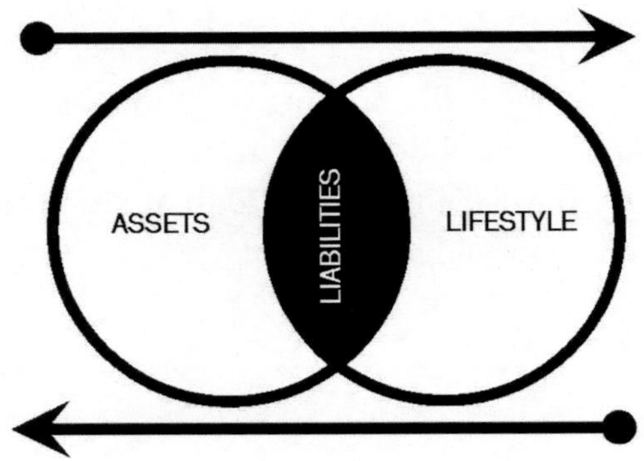

The prosperity rings illustrate the relationship between the three areas that are key to understanding fiscal stewardship and fiscal literacy. The size of your liabilities directly affects the size of your assets and lifestyle. The smaller the liability section, the larger the others have the potential of growing into.

Debt has the power to determine whether you go see the latest movie at the theater or wait until it hits TNT in a few months. Debt has the power of control, stress, peace, fun, and tension.

If you've got more month than money, you know how debt can control your life. It is critical that we see that debt is not God's plan for our lives. Take a look at the fruits of the Spirit in Galatians 5:22–23: love, joy, peace, patience, kindness, goodness, faithfulness, gentleness, and don't forget self-control.

Let's look at these one at a time:

- Debt versus love: Love for oneself that one must indulge in excessive purchases on credit to satisfy some craving.
- Debt versus joy: The only joy in debt is the joy that is robbed or the joy received by the creditor of his newfound asset.
- Debt versus peace: Have you ever met anyone completely at peace with their debt, or are they stressed out?
- Debt versus patience: Yes, debt is the fruit of a lack of patience. Buy now, pay later?

- Debt versus kindness/goodness: Taking out debt is very kind and good to the creditors, not so much to your family. If you are in debt, stress grows, usually creating a tense, angry, or frustrated person.
- Debt versus gentleness: Gentleness is a myth and legend in the debt collection world. Try to have a civilized conversation with a debt collector sometime. They want their money.
- Debt versus self-control: Debt does not represent self-control but a lack thereof.

How is any of this God's plan for us again?

Dave Ramsey puts it like this: "Personal finance is 80 percent behavior and only 20 percent head knowledge." So, in this section, let's take a look at some of the types of liabilities that get us down, as well as some of the symptoms.

Before we get started, let's define *liability*.

By the financial world, a liability is an obligation or amount owed on credit.

Robert Kiyosaki has become famous for changing the meaning of a liability to anything that takes money out of our pocket.

By this definition, Kiyosaki says the difference between the rich and the poor is how they buy what they think are assets when in fact they are liabilities.

We used your car as an example in the asset section, so let's use it again. Most people purchase cars thinking they are assets. A closer look shows that cars depreciate in huge amounts over time and require ongoing maintenance and registration annually. If you lose your income, does the car add or subtract money from your balance sheet? We established in the last section the losing venture of a car as an asset. This is not even considering a loan, just the car itself.

Now that we know what a liability is, let's look at some different types of debts to which we fall prey. Yes, I say prey. The enemy is using debt as a huge part of his attack on us. Look at these.

Credit Cards

I don't know about you, but I got my first two credit cards on campus the first week of college years ago. Do you want a shocking stat? "Eighty percent of graduating college seniors have credit card debt before they even have a job," according to Dave Ramsey in his book *The Total Money Makeover*. That is staggering.

Why are credit card companies so quick to hand out the plastic to college students without any income? They understand that their business model is all about brand loyalty. Somewhere deep in our psyche lays a desire to be "initiated" into adulthood. The first company to issue this new "plastic power" gives a rite of passage to these kids who have no idea how the use of these cards will affect their lives for many years to come. Brand loyalty is very real and is a big tool of the enemy.

To you mothers and fathers: it is more important than ever before to take the time to teach your children about the use of responsible credit management before they leave the protection of your nest. With no training, our kids are being set up to get their training from the enemy.

If you recall how monthly compound interest works, credit cards earn daily compound interest. That's right. Banks pay you compound interest monthly at low rates and earn compound interest from you daily at high rates.

We were innocent and just wanting to "build our credit." After all, everyone else is doing it. Isn't it smart to build your credit somehow? These are all issues I deal with every day in my mortgage and financial consulting practice.

Credit card companies are genius in their approach to getting us to use their cards. Think about the use of debit cards. In relation to your credit card, where do you keep them in your wallet? And what is the logo on the debit card? Visa or MasterCard, right? So when you don't have the cash in your checking account, just use the card next to it. Subtle, right? These wolves have snuck in among sheep to mock our cash accounts.

The cards are identical. Now, using a credit card is like using extra money we have access to, right? Well, every time you use the credit card, it is an instant loan. The interest monster wastes no time at eating away our wealth. Boy was that a good burger or what? I look good in these jeans, don't I? These are the best new CDs.

Credit cards are nothing but a tool that these companies, who gain most from our use, want us to believe. If you have credit cards, wage war against the habitual use of them. Pay them off and close them down. It's time to take back your financial peace and kick the enemy out of your wallet and life for good if you ever want to follow God's fiscal stewardship plan.

Please don't take this all the wrong way. I do not hate credit cards. They are good tools in certain situations. The problems lie in the lack of education on what those situations are. If you don't know how to use credit responsibly, you don't need to have the credit. It's similar to giving a gun to an inexperienced user. Wouldn't you shudder in fear if that were to occur?

Here is a solution if the habit is hard to break. Once you pay off your cards, open a no-fee checking account, one that earns you interest if possible. Deposit whatever amount you would like your credit limit to be. You may not have much money right now to start with. That's okay. Make sure the account allows use of a debit card. Now, on a monthly basis, pay yourself plus interest if that excites you. The point is, you are paying cash and replenishing your own limits. Take control.

As you have more available money, you can increase your limit or keep it where it is.

Auto Loans and Other Installment Loans

Here is another of the more popular debt instruments. In one evening of television, you will see multiple new car commercials. The sirens are singing a beautiful song that you can have a new car at a low introductory rate. Wait. They may even give you money in the form of a factory rebate to ride away in your new car. It's funny that they don't tell you the depreciation of the vehicle driving off the lot. Sure, we all know it, but do they disclose the amount you lose leaving the dealer? A $28,000 car will lose nearly $17,000 over the first few years of ownership. In four years, 60 percent of the value will vanish.

So how do these auto loans work? Most have a preset term of three, four, or five years. With the increase in car prices, we're seeing loans go out as far as seventy-two and even longer. They have a preset interest rate used to calculate the amount owed over the term. These are simple calculations. How much? How long? What rate?

Well, don't be fooled by the interest rate. Why? Let's look at a $20,000 car loan over five years at 3.9 percent. Let's find out how much interest you'll pay on this loan. If in fact you are paying 3.9 percent, it is reasonable to take the $20,000 x 3.9% to determine how much you need to pay back. Oh, but that is not how it works however. The interest on these loans is compounded.

Okay. Looking at the reality of this $20,000 loan at 3.9 percent is sixty payments at $368.43 per month. The total is $22,045.80. Hmm. So that means that there is $2,045.80 in interest. My calculator tells me this is 10.2 percent of the amount borrowed, not 3.9 percent.

Car dealers know that most people buy based on monthly payments and emotions, so that is their marketing tool. They don't sell you the car as much as they sell you the payment and how you'll feel or look driving this "rugged, go anywhere truck."

Five years ago, I bought a used 2000 Chevy Suburban. It was a few years old when we bought it. It is a two-wheel drive. It is amazing to me how many people cringe at the thought I would buy a two-wheel drive. Hello, people. Newsflash. I live in the city and drive on pavement. Why would I need a four by four in the city? I don't go out to the wilderness to climb mountains in the rugged terrain as they advertise. So many people buy more than they need due to their lack of emotional control.

Twenty thousand dollars is a hard sell, but $367 is an easy sell. All they have to do is get you emotionally attached to the car so that you will agree that $367 is not that much to your budget. Quickly, once the emotional hook is in, the salesperson moves to a dialogue about how much you can afford monthly. That's where they get you. After all, you can start enjoying the luxury of this new car today, after you sign the paperwork.

So here is the way to combat this. You've heard it said, "Cash is king." I'm going back to Dave Ramsey. Dave quoted a *USA Today* study to show that the average car payment in America is $464 over sixty-four months. Most people will carry this loan with them for life since they look to trade in for a new car about the time they pay this one off. Four hundred and sixty-four dollars per month over forty years, a normal working lifetime, compounded at an average mutual fund rate of 12 percent is $5,458,854.45. Wow!

Over $5,000,000 worth of worthless cars during your working lifetime. That is amazing.

Here's what you do. Start with the $367 from our first example. In ten months, this is $3,670 that you can buy an average used car for cash. It won't be your dream car by any means. But here's how you stagger to get the car you want. Keep saving your $367 per month. In ten months, sell your car for maybe $3,000 plus the $3,670 saved and buy a new $6,670 car. Keep saving for another ten months and you have enough to buy an $11,000 used car. This is a very reliable used car that has already depreciated. The best part is no monthly payments and no debt.

Now keep driving this car as long as you can and buy yourself another used car in a few years, paying cash. You will always get a killer deal paying cash. Discounts are few and far between when buying on credit.

Practice patience, as the ant, if you want to build true wealth. Many millionaires do not buy new cars. They buy one to two year-old cars that have depreciated the most and then use cash. Then they drive them for as long as they possibly can.

The millionaires driving around in big fancy cars and mansions and furs are minority among millionaires. You don't know it, but the largest percentage of millionaires live in modest homes and drive modest cars. They don't dress elaborately and don't draw attention to themselves.

Leasing cars is never a good idea when it comes to fiscal stewardship. Unless you are on vacation and need a short-term rental, avoid these scams like the plague. These deals are set up to sell a lower monthly payment and appeal to more people. Don't get lured into a deal like this. If you have to lease a car to afford the payment on the nice car for status, your life is shaping up to be a fantasy you can't afford.

Twelve Months Same as Cash

These loans are set up by marketing people to sell cars, furniture, jewelry, and electronics. Creditors know that if they give you a period like twelve months or six months same as cash, 88 percent of these deals convert to debt. When these loans convert to debt, all of the interest or "finance charge" accrued during the twelve months is backdated and added back to the note if not paid off in the prescribed time frame.

I learned this the hard way while in college. I bought a $2,000 computer with a twelve-month same as cash deal. I sent just over $100 per month for 12 months. On the thirteenth month, I expected a $900 bill since I was diligently making my payments. My bill shot up to over $1,900! They added a year's worth of interest to my bill when I didn't have it paid off in the twelve months. Same as cash is what they get, not the consumer. Beware of these promotions.

The idea is to use OPM or other people's money. Well, the problem is that the wealthy never use these loans. They walk in and pay cash to negotiate a lower deal. A car with no interest for several months may not be charging you any interest, but you're driving off the lot losing thousands in depreciation. If you think you can make the $200 bucks a month on the $2,400 living room set to pay it off in twelve months, save the $200 a month for ten months and walk in to negotiate a lower deal. Not only will you not get caught in the interest trap, you'll probably be able to save ten to twenty percent off the sales price. That is savings. Pay cash. Cash is king.

Debt Consolidation Loans

These loans may or may not be a good idea. The idea here is to take a loan to pay off other debt at a lower interest rate and new terms. Yes, many times, there are monthly savings in payments. Don't be fooled by this. Most of the savings is because the term is spread out over more time. The overall interest paid is higher over time.

Many studies done by debt consolidation companies show that 78 percent of the people who take out these loans replace the debt within a very short period of time.

How is that so? Think about it. You fall into one of two groups. You have either done one of these loans or you know someone who has. The most common phrase when doing one of these loans is, "We just paid off all of our debts." Here is a red flag statement. No. You restructured and moved your debt. You still have it and still owe it.

How do you avoid this trap? If you pay off all of your debt in a plan like this, do one of two things with the extra monthly savings. Either save the money in an investment we discussed in the asset section or apply it to the new consolidation loan to get rid of it faster and save on the long-term interest.

Don't be fooled by the thought that you've gotten rid of your debt. It is a myth and fantasy, another trick by the enemy to keep you trapped and slave to the master creditor.

"The rich rule over the poor, and the borrower is servant to the lender," (Prov. 22:7).

Debts and liabilities make the one who owes a slave or servant. How hard is it to serve the Lord if you are a slave to money? Didn't Jesus warn us that we can only serve one master, either God or money?

Yes, I do believe one of the most important parts of our service to the Lord is having the self-control to avoid the money traps of the devil. He wants to have you. Remember that he tempted the Lord with riches and kingdoms of the world.

Do you remember Jesus' reply? "Get away from me!" Debt is a way to get what we can't afford. Remember, he who is good with a little will be blessed with much according to the parable of the ten minas.

Credit Report

Another area to take control when thinking about debt and liabilities is your credit report. Credit reporting is a snapshot of how well you've performed with the credit obligations you've agreed to. This is also your financial reputation.

Credit reports have been a mystery for many years. Today, there is so much information available on the Internet to make you an expert in credit reports.

There are only five things that affect credit scores:

- 35 percent—Payment history: Do you pay your bills on time? Thirty days behind? Don't agree with a creditor's decision to charge for something you didn't do? This is the easiest part of your credit score to manage. Pay on time! Collections, legal judgments, bankruptcy, and late payments all fall into this category. Yes, over one third of your credit score is affected by this one category. A thirty-day late payment can be extremely harmful.

- 30 percent—Amounts owed: This is how you use your credit cards. Do you run the limits up to the max on a regular occasion? This hurts your score by 30 percent. Keeping the balances on your credit cards below 30 percent of what is available maximizes this part of your score. A little patience and self control and this is very easy to manage.
- 15 percent—Length of credit history: This is the average age of all your credit accounts. Only time can help you on this one. It's not always the best practice to close accounts when they're not in use, as it can affect your average age of the history. This factor looks at the age of open credit accounts.
- 10 percent—Types of credit: Spread the wealth, they say—Credit cards, installment loans, mortgages, car loans, etc. The more diverse your credit shows signs of responsible borrowing.
- 10 percent—New credit or inquiries: Any time you open new credit or a creditor reviews your credit. The myth says that this is a fast way to pull your scores down. Keep in mind that this is only 10 percent of your total score and has little bearing. If the other areas are not so strong, this will impact your scores on a larger scale.

By understanding what is in your credit, you can make smarter decisions about managing and maximizing your credit scores. In the world of credit, a score greater than

720 is king. You will get the best deals when the need to borrow does come up.

Manage this little number, and you can save thousands in interest charges.

Compound Interest

Remember the charts we looked at in the asset section regarding compound interest? Well, we don't need to spend much time on this. Keep in mind that if you're not receiving interest, you're paying it (usually at a higher rate and compounded more frequently).

Why is this important? When looking at your assets, your biggest ally is time. When considering debt, time is your biggest enemy.

So let's look at the time value of money.

Time Value of Money

Age 25	$ 5,000.00	6% (12 Yr)	Age 25	$ 5,000.00	10% (7.2 Yr)
37	$ 10,000.00		32	$ 10,000.00	
49	$ 20,000.00		39	$ 20,000.00	
61	$ 40,000.00		46	$ 40,000.00	
73	$ 80,000.00		53	$ 80,000.00	
			60	$ 160,000.00	
			67	$ 320,000.00	
			74	$ 640,000.00	

Do you see how understanding the time value of compounded interest is important to the future value of your assets and your liabilities? Whose asset is growing here? Clue: not yours.

This is not rocket science. It is simply math. If you understand how this works, you can make it work to your advantage. God will bless and prosper you when you know how this simple law works.

In closing, remembering the importance of managing your liabilities will directly impact your lifestyle and your ability to save building future wealth. Any fault in the area of liabilities directly robs your future.

Take a look at Benjamin Franklin's words of wisdom:

- A penny saved is a penny earned.
- A man may—if he knows not how to save as he gets—keep his nose to the grindstone.
- When the well is dry, they know the worth of water.
- For age and want, save while you may; no morning sun lasts a whole day.
- He that burns logs that cost nothing is twice warmed.
- If you would be wealthy, think of saving as well as of getting.
- Beware of little Expenses; a small leak will sink a great ship.
- A fat kitchen makes a lean will.
- Fools make Feasts, and wise men eat them.
- What maintains one vice, would bring up two children.

Let's take a look at a very simple plan to eliminate all of your debt in the shortest amount of time. This is not the only way to eliminate debt, but it is certainly a very popular method for the people who have used it.

The Debt Snowball

I'm going back to Dave Ramsey and the very simple plan that he and many other credit and debt counseling agencies use to help thousands of families, including Dave himself, eliminate the debts in their lives in a relatively short period of time.

The bottom line is that if you don't have any monthly debt payments, wealth is easy to acquire. I am going to include the worksheets the debt snowball worksheet to show you how easy it can be. I'm not saying it won't be challenging because it will. I am saying that it is simple, not easy if you take it on. You will be required to provide more effort than you've had to do in any other venture you've taken on financially.

Do you remember how we started out the chapter? Personal finance is 80 percent behavior and 20 percent head knowledge. Follow the instructions on the debt snowball worksheet to bear the fruit.

The Debt Snowball

List your debts in order with the smallest payoff or balance first. Do not be concerned with interest rates or terms unless two debts have similar payoffs; then list the higher interest rate debt first. Paying the little debts off first gives you quick feedback, and you are more likely to stay with the plan.

Redo this sheet each time you pay off a debt so that you can see how close you are getting to freedom. Keep the old sheets to wallpaper the bathroom in your new debt-free house. The "new payment" is found by adding all the payments on the debts listed above that item to the payment you are working on so that you have compounding payments that will get you out of debt very quickly. "Payments remaining" is the number of payments remaining when you get down the snowball to that item. "Cumulative Payments" is the total payments needed, including the snowball, to pay off that item. In other words, this is your running total for "payments remaining."

Countdown to Freedom

Date: ____________________________

Item Payoff	Total Payment	Minimum Payment	New Payment	Payment Remaining	Cumulative Payments

Lifestyle Management

Go to the ant, you sluggard; consider its ways and be wise! It has no commander, no overseer or ruler, yet it stores its provisions in summer and gathers food at harvest. A little sleep a little slumber, a little folding of the hands to rest—and poverty will come on you like a bandit and scarcity like an armed man.

Proverbs 6:6–11 (NIV)

Not long after that, the younger son got together all he had, set off for a distant country and there squandered his wealth in wild living. After he had spent everything, there was a severe famine in that whole country, and he began to be in need.

Luke 15:13–14 (NIV)

Do you remember the drawing we learned about in the last two sections on assets and liabilities?

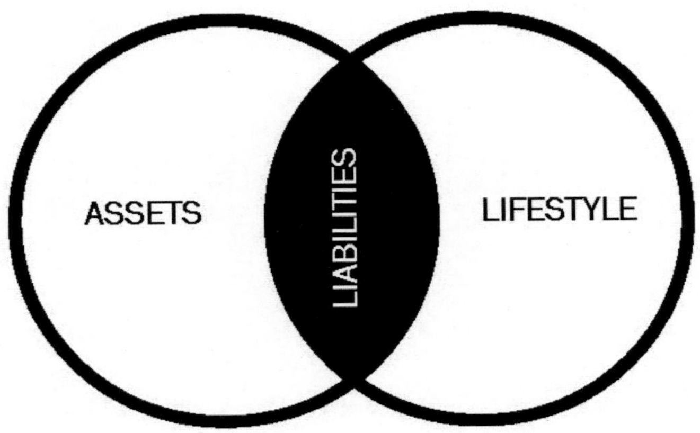

Now take a closer look at the relationship between the assets, the liabilities, and lifestyle. In this section, we are going to study lifestyle choices that affect our assets and liabilities.

Looking closer at the relationship of each of these important areas in your life, notice that the larger the liability section becomes the smaller each of the other becomes.

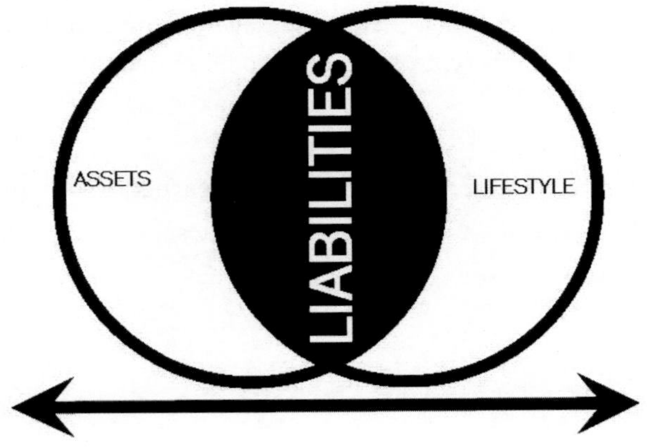

And the opposite is true. If you truly want to have a significant and abundant lifestyle with plenty of assets, you'll need fewer liabilities to accomplish this.

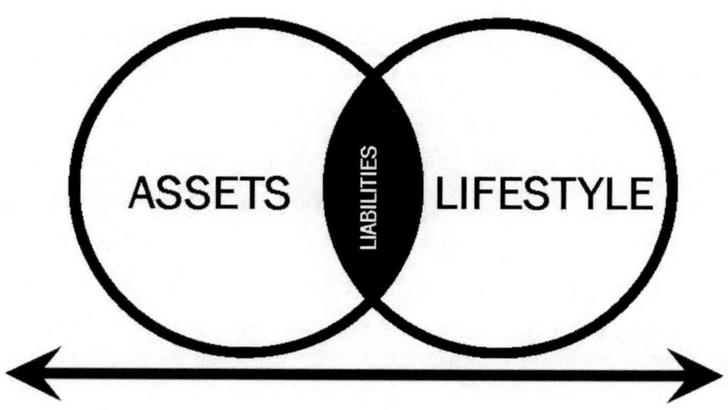

Do you remember television shows like *The Lifestyles of the Rich and Famous*, *Dallas*, *The Hills*, or *The Apprentice*? All of these programs showcase the glamorous riches of characters who have nothing better to do than fight over money and wild living. They set the tone for a great lie that Americans have fallen prey to. Can you guess what the lie is?

I love the way Dave Ramsey put it in his book, *The Total Money Makeover*. He says that many people get money, only to come down with a terrible case of "affluenza." That's right, "affluenza."

Affluenza is a plague overtaking our country like the locusts on Egypt. It is simply the idea driven by the compulsive need for more status through the acquisition of things. Guess how we go about acquiring these things? That's right. Through credit cards and personal loans.

Most Americans cannot afford to live the lavish lifestyles that they portray day in and day out.

The lifestyle choices we make ultimately determine the lifestyle we will have. Let's take a minute to look at a few of these ideas.

Cars. Have you seen the latest Acura, Hummer, or BMW hitting the street? What about the return of muscle? The Camaro, Mustang, and Charger have hit the scene attracting retiring baby boomers back to the glory days of their youth. Shoot. I'm not a baby boomer, and my motor gets a little revved up by the muscle on the street.

Movies like *Gone in* 60 *Seconds* and *The Fast and the Furious* glamorize cars and make them out to be almost godlike. Come on, guys. Tell me you don't get just a little warm under the collar when Nicholas Cage walks up to Eleanor (the 68 Shelby fast back). I did. What about Vin Diesel's all-American Mopar at the end of *The Fast and the Furious* which is returning to the big screen in the fourth installment of the series this spring.

Cars have a way of alluring us into finance offices to sign our lives away. Have you ever wanted heads to turn when they see you pull up in your new ride? How about this one? Have you ever slowed down in front of a glass building to catch your own reflection driving your "hot" ride? It's embarrassing to say, but I've done it. What about the rev of the engine next to your buddies at a stoplight.

So the hook is set. The need is a feeling of status. Affluenza is winning the battle. The look is one of success and power.

We go into the bank or finance department at the car

dealer. We walk out feeling like a million bucks because we got our new dream for only $300 per month. Shoot! That's nothing. I can do $300 a month in my sleep.

It's Friday. We get in our new car and head to the mall for the new clothes to fit the image we've just created for ourselves. But because we don't have any money and payday is a week away, we use Mr. Visa. Oh wait. There's a 10 percent discount if I get the department store card. Well, this is an unusual event. Since I am spending $500 on new clothes, I should get the $50 off. I'll pay it off next week when I get paid. No problem, we tell ourselves.

When we get together with our friends, they start asking what type of wheels we're going to put on the new car. Oh, I hadn't thought of that. Let's head down to the tire shop and pick some out. So you spend Saturday morning getting the new rims and wheels put on the car. Twelve hundred dollars and another credit card later, you've got shiny new bling, bling rims and wheels that are surely turning the heads.

Monday rolls around and you remember that you've got to call the insurance agent to get your new car insured. Well, this car is brand-new, and the agent needs a deposit on the new insurance of $300 and $95 per month. You think, *Well I'm supposed to pay off the credit card next week when I get paid, but I've really got to pay this bill now or my car won't be covered if something happens.* So you put off the credit card expense.

A month has gone by, and you don't know why you're running short of cash. You can't imagine where the money has gone. Well, let's see. You started out with $500 in discretionary income before you bought your new car. Your old car got great gas mileage and was paid for with very inexpensive insurance. Now you have a $300 per month car payment, a $50 credit card payment, $75 tire payments, and $95 insurance payments, not to mention the amount of gas required to drive around showing off the new car to all of your friends.

Every time someone wants to go somewhere, it's another opportunity to show off the new car. Of course, you have to volunteer to drive. Your monthly gas bill hits $200 per month.

Oops. That's right. You're over budget. How did that happen? Well, it looks like we'll have to use the credit cards for a little while to figure this all out. Gas and food start going on the credit card. The $3 per gallon is now $4.25 a gallon because we can't pay the card off at the end of the month.

You start to think about areas you can shave. First is the 401k contribution. If we drop that from 10 percent to 5 percent, we've got an extra $250 per month. We can start it up again after we figure this out.

You can see how very quickly it sets in and can mess up an entire financial plan or lack thereof. If your financial plan is reliant upon some future event kicking in, you're in trouble.

Go back and review the power of compound interest. Your lifestyle "needs" just traded your compound interest for the credit card and bank's compound interest plan (which I promise is better than yours to begin with).

Although this illustration is a bit "out there" and you're probably saying to yourself, *I'd never do that,* ask yourself this. Do you finance your car? Do you have the set in belief that you'll always have a car payment? Many people have this one set in. Too many miles? Trade it in for the new one. After all, it's more reliable. The truth is that there is nothing wrong with the car you're driving except it's not new.

Better yet. Do you lease a car? Car leases allow you to spend less per month and about three times what the car is not worth in the first place. Do you have a wallet full of credit cards that are for "emergency use" only? Then why do you have them in your wallet? Eating out is not an emergency. Travel is not an emergency.

Do you know that airline miles are very rarely redeemed? Card companies say that over 70 percent of the miles acquired are never redeemed. Wake up and stop the madness! If you don't travel and don't use the miles, you're not doing yourself any favors.

Managing your lifestyle is the hardest and most critical part of financial success. Do you remember the idea that 80 percent of financial success is based on your habits? Your future depends on you paying for it today. The problem is that too many of us are paying for our past today and for today tomorrow. That's all good and fine today while you have an income. The problem will hit you sometime in your mid fifties when you want to retire but won't have the means to do it.

I hear Walmart greeters get a great benefits package. Seriously, is that what you're working for? Your retirement plan is to play and pay for yesterday only to retire and work more at a job where you don't want to be?

Please don't get me wrong. There are some very good people who hold that job at Walmart. I'm grateful that Walmart has a sense to help out our seniors in their later years. You can make different choices today to create a different retirement plan. It is not too late to start.

You've got to take this very seriously. Our culture of the American dream is a lie. I am very passionate about this. I got caught up in it myself. I'm paying today for yesterday's choices. I will tell you this. I am not happy about it and will be out of my mess in a short time to start planning wholeheartedly for my family's future.

The American dream is not, "Let's see who has the most debt." The American lie is "Buy now, pay later." You don't believe me? Start watching your TV commercials—twelve months same as cash; no payments, no interest until February 2013; zero percent balance transfers for six months. Furniture, cars, and jewelry have the biggest "savings" scams out there.

If I remember, the American dream is to *own* a home and prosper. All of these lifestyle entitlements are eating up the monthly budget and America's future prosperity. Don't forget that this is not God's plan of prosperity for your life. This is your plan. It's time to learn a little self-discipline.

If you want to get ahead in this culture, you've got to stop believing the lies about having things.

I am a product of generation X. My parents tell me stories about their childhood. My father grew up on a farm in Iowa. My mother grew up in a farming community and worked in the fields during her summer breaks. If you've ever been around farms, there is a lot of work to be done. Work ethics were taught, and farmers who don't save lose their farms to the banks when a bad season hits them.

Generation X is a defining generation. We live in a time

when PS2, Xbox, microwave ovens, personal computers, cable television, and cell phones are not luxuries but normal events. We've seen these things come about in our lifetimes.

I remember thinking that the kid down the street with the Atari was the coolest kid on the block. Now if you don't have an Xbox, gaming system, or Internet service, you're a little weird by most standards today. Not twenty-five years ago. It was rare to have these game systems. Today, people are playing these games on their portable cell phones and Nintendo DS.

I remember a time when Internet was rarely available at home, so we went to the library for free access. To consider doing that today is a crime to mention. How could someone possibly suggest not having Internet at home?

Our society and culture have made Internet, cell phones and cable television a "need" when really they are wants and luxuries. If you can't afford them, it is your responsibility to make different choices.

See, lifestyle is all about choices. Starting every morning, we all make choices of how we are going to dress, what Starbucks drink we'll have today, did we pack our lunch or will we eat out with friends? What's for dinner, Dominoes or Pizza Hut? Should we meet our friends for "happy hour" to commiserate about the days events? (Now there's an oxy-moron.)

Dreams? What dreams? Who can afford them without a credit card? No one can if the debt monster and the lie we call life doesn't destroy every dream we've ever had. I know older people who stopped dreaming years ago.

In fact, look at the midlife crisis that sets in somewhere around forty years old. Is this phenomenon a product of living a life we're not happy with because we gave up on our dreams? Let's tackle that one in another book on another day.

Your income is your biggest wealth-building tool. However, most of our society makes choices to forfeit a little bit of our future wealth to finance yesterday's play date. Go for it. All I can say is if these are your choices, stop whining about them and take some responsibility.

Was the housing crisis the mortgage company's fault, the president's fault, Wall Street's fault, or Fannie Mae's fault? I will go so far as to say that all of these parties made mistakes along the way and definitely took advantage of unsuspecting consumers. That's the problem. Consumers were *unsuspecting*.

The banking system has some very big problems to say the least. Let's face it. At the end of the day, if consumers didn't buy these loans, they never would have been written. It is time, as a Christian before God, for each and every one of us to start taking responsibility for the Lifestyle choices we make.

Oh, don't get me wrong on this one. I am a living, breathing example of the mortgage industry mishap. Not only did I take a loan with no income verification. I also earn my living in the industry. I do not, however, blame anyone for the choices I made that landed my family in the financial mess we hit last year. No. I made these choices.

By saying that it is the mortgage company's fault or Washington, DC, that I lost my home and filed bankruptcy is a forfeiture of my intelligence as a human being.

No mortgage company and no Washington congressman made my financial choices.

See, it is here in this place right now that I'm going to get abrupt and direct. Take some responsibility. We were all born into this world with nothing, and we will all leave this world with nothing. The only things we have in the middle are the choices we make.

If you don't like where you are today, choose a different road. No one is forcing you to take the road you're on. God has given everyone of us an intelligent mind to make smart choices. He created every one of us in his image. It is time that we start to act as if we are made in his image. It is time that we start to ask the question of our lifestyle as if it was God himself making the choice.

It's not your boss's fault or your spouse's fault or your parent's fault that *you* signed your life away in debt. It's not your boss's fault that *you* accepted the position paying what it pays. It's not the car salesman's fault that *you* wanted a new car. The bank is not responsible for making your payments, so don't yell at them when they are trying to collect what *you* agreed to pay back.

Lifestyle is about choices. I can't stress this enough. You don't believe me? Look at the two passages beginning this chapter. One is about an ant who labors every day to store up provisions for future events. If you choose to finish reading the passage, the second half is a comparison of the ant to the sluggard or, as one translation puts it, a lazy man. Well, guess what, my friend. If you're living in a world of debt, it is a sign of sluggardlike tendencies.

You may not like it, but a sluggard wants without

working for it. A sluggard cuts corners. A sluggard buys when he should not buy. A sluggard vacations with borrowed money. A sluggard is the most deceptive of all creatures. He lives his life creating a false sense of security for himself and, worst of all, for his family. Then he has the audacity to blame others for his misfortune. There is no misfortune at play, only a series of choices.

Look at the next passage from Luke. The parable of the lost son is a great story on many levels. Carefully review the two sons. The eldest son does everything the father asks and more. The younger son squanders his inheritance. One has a humble attitude. One has an entitlement attitude. One has the attitude of scarcity. The story does not show how long it took the father to amass his fortune. It also doesn't tell us how quickly the son squandered his inheritance. The point is, what choices are you making with what you've been given to manage?

The choices you make determine the course of your life. Fear and trepidation ruin financial success. Wild living and squandering also bring about financial ruin.

I already mentioned that more than 50 percent of all millionaires drive cars that are two or more years old? The men on average do not spend more than $500 on their suits or $150 on their shoes. Most millionaires don't even wear expensive watches. The average millionaire home in America is worth about $350,000 and has very little to no mortgage on it.

Frugality, not poverty, is a sign of a millionaire mindset.

Do I tell you all this so that you can run out and amass a fortune, not enjoying life? Absolutely not. Let's spend the last half of this chapter talking about some choices that will put you over the top.

Drive your car into the ground, and pay cash for your next one. The average person will spend over $2,000,000 on cars in their forty to fifty-year adult life. Most of that is in interest expense to the bank. If you take forty years and divide it by eight, that gives you five cars for eight years each. Let's say you pay $20,000 per car. That is only $100,000 versus $2,000,000. Wow! Look at that. I just gave you a $1.9 million dollar raise.

Hmm. That'll make you think a little. Do you think buying two to three year-old cars and driving them for eight years is realistic? Most cars will last anywhere from 150–200,000 miles. If you purchase the car with 40,000 miles and drive 20,000 per year, that pretty much takes you right out to the 200,000-mile mark. All you really have to do is maintain the car.

So how do you pay cash for cars? Try this. Once you pay off your car with the $400 payments, keep paying yourself $400 per month for the next five years. Guess what. You've got $24,000 in principal (not including compound interest you earn) and plenty to buy a "new" used car. Then keep up the trend. If you continue the $400 for the next eight years, you will have $38,400 not including compounded interest. Wait a minute. After only two cycles of this, you've got money left over to invest in the future. Just don't stop paying yourself the $400 per month.

Trust me. If you stay on the car ownership plan most people have, you'll be paying more than $400 per month for the rest of your life every time you finance a car. Most people finance a car for five years only to trade it in to finance another for five more years. Well, you can see where this is going.

It's all about choices.

What about lattes? David Bach, author of *Automatic Millionaire*, shares a great idea he calls the latte factor. Are you someone who stops by Starbucks every morning on the way to work? Removing weekends, there are twenty to twenty-one working days in a month. Using twenty days and $4.81 per day as a cost of a latte, you slowly leak $96.20 every month on lattes.

Well, $96.20 over thirty years (simple math, not considering inflation for the latte) is $34,632 worth of lattes. What if you were to invest only half of the $96.20 or $48.10 per month into a monthly-compounded interest account at 8 percent? $72,212 is the end effect of "sacrificing" half of your latte pleasure. You don't even have to give up the latte.

What's that? Did I just give you another $72,000 raise for your lifetime?

Have you considered the cost of smoking? The average pack of cigarettes is over $3.00 today. Let's look at the cost of smoking for thirty years. The average smoker smokes one and half packs per day using thirty days in a month. That is $135 dollars per month or $48,600 over thirty years, not figuring in inflation. Keep in mind that the health issues related to smoking will eventually cost more in medical expenses over your lifetime.

Well, the same $135 per month compounded monthly at 8 percent works out to be $202,675 over thirty years. I'm telling you. Here's another raise for you. Two hundred thousand dollars to spend in retirement? Whatever will you do?

Don't thank me yet. There's more.

What if your family of four eats out? I know that when I've done the math for my family, it works out to about $300–350 per month eating out. It kinda makes me wonder why we ever bought groceries. Well, cut that number down to $150 per month. What do you think thirty years of eating out (not adjusted for inflation) is? If you stay on your current path of $300 per month, you'll spend over $108,000 over thirty years.

Take the $150 savings over thirty years at 8 percent and let's see what that works out to be: $225,194. Amazing what can happen in a lifetime if you know the numbers. Yes, that's right. Here's yet another $225,000 raise for you, my friend.

Let's go back to the big one in the car. We already looked at how you can pay cash for the car. What is the value of paying cash over forty years if you pay yourself every month $400 and earn 8 percent? You will save yourself $1.4 million dollars over forty years on that plan. Keep in mind that this number does not take into account removing $20,000 every five years to pay cash for a new car.

Assume all of the examples I just used represent a real life. What type of salary would it take to cover these? Housing of $1,200 per month plus car insurance of $35 per month plus credit card payments of $250 per month plus groceries of $400 per month plus a car payment of $400 per month plus Starbucks of $96.20 per month plus cigarettes of $135 per month plus eating out at $300 per month plus gas for the car of $250 per month plus other miscellaneous items of $150 per month. A net amount of $3,216.20 per month, or if you figure 35 percent for taxes and insurance, a gross amount of $4,948 or $59,376 per year for a household income. That is a very average household income in America.

Keep in mind that none of the utilities, cable, phones, etc. are figured in here. You get the illustration though.

Living the average lifestyle of most Americans will cost you over $2 million toward a very healthy retirement. Simple choices. I didn't tell you to cut out everything. Simply reduce your habitual spending activity and keep more of the money you're already spending during your week.

Before reading this, would you have thought it possible to become a millionaire in your lifetime, making a household income of $60,000 per year? Using the examples above, there is an extra $733 dollars every month being wasted frivolously on things that will easily make you a millionaire.

If you are thirty years old, this takes you out to age sixty. Well, if you're still working, you'll have more. Just a few adjustments can make all the difference at the end.

Keep in mind that all of these calculations are used to illustrate and do not represent accurate projections. There is no inflation calculated into prices. There are also no income increases calculated into this equation. If you are smart with your taxes, there are a ton of exemptions and deductions you can take to pay less in taxes on your income.

Using inflation as a projection, you will need approximately $8.3 million dollars to retire comfortably in thirty years to be able to last another twenty-five years without working. Even with all of the savings, there are many other things you will need to employ to ensure the ability to retire with a little dignity by age of sixty-five.

The point I want to be very clear on is this: there is an enemy among us, wanting us to believe we need all of these "nice" things and that financing them is no big deal. I hope you now see that it is a *huge* deal.

Do you now see how the choices you make will either create liabilities or assets. You have to decide which you prefer. When you make your choice, own it. If your choice is not the one that properly stores away provisions for your future, then take responsibility for the choices *you* make.

If your spouse makes a lot of choices without you, then *stop* it from happening. If you allow it to continue, that is your choice. No more whining. Work as a team, and store up your provisions together. By the way, two working smart are far better than one.

Here is another staggering statistic. Eighty-five percent of graduating college students have $5,000 or more of credit card debt and no job. Nineteen percent of all the bankruptcies in 2006 were filed by college students. Hello, people! Wake up! These are our kids. Where did they learn their financial habits? Do I need to answer that question?

Did you know that it costs about $5,000 more per year for a student to live off campus and eat out than it does on campus in the dorms and cafeteria? Well, guess where all of the student loans go? It's not rocket science. That is an additional $20,000 in loans to cover living off campus. A good state school will cost less than $30,000 to attend if you finish in four years. That is sixteen credits per semester for eight semesters or 128 hours for a bachelor's degree. Guess what. Thirty thousand dollars is $3,750 per semester.

At least in New Mexico, a semester of college at UNM is $2285.40 for tuition and about $450 for books. Now that doesn't include housing and living expenses, but your student is going to pay these whether he is in school or not. Clearly, $3,750 is more than enough to cover tuition and books. In fact, a four-year degree should run somewhere around $22-$24,000.

It is time that we stand up and start fighting for our children's future now. If you don't have children but plan on having them, college is a huge step for them. Managing your lifestyle is no longer just about you.

It is time that we start honoring both God and our families with the choices we make in our lives. No one else is doing it for you.

Do you remember these words Jesus spoke?

> The thief comes only to steal and kill and destroy; I have come that they may have life, and have it to the full.
>
> John 10:10 (NIV)

Jesus did not come to give us a life of bondage and slavery to the lender. He came to give us life, and a good one at that.

There is a thief and an enemy that is out to get each of us. His intention is to steal from us, kill us, and destroy us. We are under constant attack, so remember that the choices you make every single day are either adding fuel to his fire or they are setting you free to live life to the *full.*

You decide! It's *your* choice.

Renting versus Buying

Go to the ant, you sluggard; consider its ways and be wise! It has no commander, no overseer or ruler, yet it stores its provisions in summer and gathers food at harvest. A little sleep a little slumber, a little folding of the hands to rest—and poverty will come on you like a bandit and scarcity like an armed man.

Proverbs 6:6–11 (NIV)

All the believers were together and had everything in common. Selling their possessions and goods, they gave to anyone as he had need. Every day they continued to meet together in the temple courts. They broke bread in their homes and ate together with glad and sincere hearts, praising God and enjoying the favor of all the people.

Acts 2:44–47 (NIV)

There were no needy persons among them. For from time to time those who owned lands or houses sold them, brought the money from the sales

> and put it at the apostles' feet, and it was distributed to anyone as he had need.
>
> Acts 4:34–35 (NIV)

So what's the big deal with buying a house?

Jesus did, after all, send out the seventy-two in Luke's account (Luke 10) to towns with no money, food, or place to stay. It was about their faith. If someone accepted one of the seventy-two in peace, they were to stay at that house with that person. If they were not accepted, they were to wipe their feet of dust and leave the town.

Jesus called us to follow him and imitate what he did. We know from the scriptures that Jesus stayed with people in their homes as well as sleeping in the wilderness. He did not buy houses or even have a forwarding address. Where did his mail go? How did people know where he was? (Don't answer that.)

I don't know about you, but the idea that Jesus told us he had no place to lay his head while the foxes and birds have a home confuses me a bit.

If Jesus didn't have a place to lay his head, should we even consider buying a home, or should we rent and remain ready to move if called? That really is the question.

Didn't Jesus tell the rich ruler (Luke 18:18–30,) to sell all of his possessions, give to the poor, and follow him? It doesn't mention a house. Jesus was going after the man's heart on the issue of inheriting the kingdom of God. I've actually heard preachers use this dialogue to discourage home ownership. Jesus wanted the rich man, who was very attached to his possessions, to put nothing before

Jesus as his Lord. Unfortunately, Luke recorded that the rich young man left sad.

Well, the goal of this chapter is to help you make this important decision. I will not tell you it is right or wrong to rent or buy. This is a decision you must make for yourself according to your faith. I can only share the Scriptures God gave us on the matter and allow the Spirit to help you in your decision.

Along the way, I will share different ideas about home ownership in the context of a financial plan as well as fiscal stewardship.

Personally, I wrestled with the very thought of buying my first home. I wrestled with the idea that I may be robbing God and living a worldly life if I wanted to have a material possession like a home. I lived under the notion that renting was the best way to imitate Jesus and the best way to stay flexible if called to move for the Lord.

My prayer, as you read these pages, is that the Lord will reveal to you the best path for your life. With that, let's review some of the benefits of owning a home.

Owning a Home

So, you think you want to buy a house? Let's see what it takes to buy a home.

In my profession, I help people with their mortgage financing. You may not know what a mortgage is, so we will look at this important tool used to help buy a home.

First, let's see what it takes to buy a home. Buying a home is one of the key factors that make up the American dream. People flock to the United States every year to own a small piece of land and a home they can call home.

Years ago, a client of mine said, "A house is just a house. It only becomes a home when it is filled with memories." I do not remember the client's name, but I hope he knows I can't claim that nugget myself. Whether renting or owning, a home is comprised of years of memories.

Isn't that so true though? When was the last time you set up your Christmas tree at the park? Do you remember racing down the street to find presents under a parked car? How about sleepovers? They sure are fun down by the river. Backyard barbeques? Family reunions? Did you ever wonder where 99 percent of the pictures for cheesy Christmas cards sent out each year are taken? Most are in someone's home.

Do your parents or grandparents ever tell you to "come home" to visit once in a while?

Sure they do. These are all very common events in our lives that are done within the walls of a home—of your home.

Where did the early Christians eat their meals with glad and sincere hearts? In their homes, daily. Can you imagine the incredible relationships these early disciples had with one another?

In any of these cases, do you remember the home or the memories built within the walls of the home? No. Your memories are of the events that take place within those walls.

Wasn't it Peter's house where Jesus stayed early in his ministry? Do you remember the great stressful meal shared with Jesus at Martha and Mary's house? What about the night Mary threw herself at Jesus' feet in Simon the Pharisee's house over dinner?

What did the early disciples sell to provide for needs within the fellowship? Possessions, goods, land, and houses are what Luke told us in Acts.

In Deuteronomy 8:10–17, the Lord is very clear to make sure we don't place our possessions over him and forget him "when we build fine houses and settle down…" He admonishes us and reminds us to remember that it is not by the power of our hands but "it is he who gives us the ability to produce wealth…"

These are very important pieces to the puzzle. Jesus told us to imitate him. He didn't own a home. Throughout the scriptures, we are given many examples of God's people who owned homes and used them to his glory.

There are warnings God places on homeownership.

"Then the word of the Lord came through the prophet Haggai: 'Is it a time for you yourselves to be living in your paneled houses, while this house (the Lord's house) remains a ruin?'"

By no means should owning a home ever get in the way of our glory given to God. Nor should homeownership ever be the end all.

Home ownership is a very emotional event and has great power in control of how we think about things going on around us. Consider some of the things we do in emotional response to our homes.

Home Depot and Lowe's are rapidly changing the face of remodeling. It used to be a community's job to make changes to a home. Remodeling has progressed from a professional's job to do the work where now we can take free classes to learn how to lay tile or paint.

Have you known someone who had a water heater go out, causing flooding? Did you see the faces of all the people in the gulf coast region who lost homes in Katrina? Have you heard their cries of everything they lost? Have you ever known anyone who bought his first home? There are expressions you'll never forget.

The first home Belinda and I bought, we entered alone with no possessions. Yes, I carried her across the threshold. We walked around from room to room, touching walls, smiling. I lay down on my carpet and rolled around. We smelled. We even looked at each other and assured one another that this little beat-up, cinder block "palace" was ours.

Take a kid like me who grew up in apartments and rental homes moving at least once per year for many years. This was a miracle from God that we owned a home. You had better believe that we told everyone we knew about it. We invited people over for cookouts, boxing matches, game nights, weekend retreats from out of town, Bible studies, you name it.

We built these memories in our home. My very first remodeling happened in that little home. Since then, we've owned two other homes, with more on the horizon.

There is something magical about owning a home that the Lord does to bring about a man's confidence. It is something magical. A certain pride of ownership happens.

Yes, homeownership has its positive and negative factors. It holds with it both blessings and curses. It's important to know what you're getting in to when you take this jump.

Mortgages

Oh boy! Here is a fun word. This is a French word that means "to death." Many get confused by a mortgage. A mortgage is not a loan. It is a legal document recorded with the county that gives a lender certain rights to the collateral (the house) as described in the document. In the event the borrower does not make proper payments on the loan, the bank can foreclose on the house and regain ownership.

When we sit down with homebuyers to sign the loan documents, the actual mortgage (sixteen pages of legalese) is described like this, "You pay, you stay. You don't, you won't."

So what's the big deal with getting a mortgage? Well, let's not focus so much on the mortgage, but let's take a look at the loan itself. Real estate is one of the most sound investment choices a person can consider. Let's look at this example. I'll compare stock to a house for the purpose of the illustration.

If you have $10,000 you want to invest in stock, you give the broker $10,000, and he gives you a certificate of stock worth $10,000. This is a simple dollar for dollar exchange until the market takes its toll. You might consider this type of speculative investing with a high hope of your $10,000 gaining more value over time.

Now, look at taking the same $10,000 and purchasing a house. The bank will help you make your purchase through this "mortgage loan." Typically, the bank wants a 5 percent down payment. So your $10,000 will "leverage" a $200,000 house. How cool is that? That's right. Your $10,000 buys an asset now worth $200,000. Historically, houses appreciate in value, giving an internal rate of return of 6 percent (typically)on a national average.

I live in Albuquerque, New Mexico. In 2007, the entire city's metropolitan statistical area (includes all surrounding cities) showed a 7.5 percent appreciation. Taken by neighborhood, the numbers vary widely. The United States as a whole did not fare as well. As a country, average appreciation was down, meaning depreciation occurred on average more often than appreciation. By far, this is an anomaly. The country averages over time about 6 percent.

So, on average, a $200,000 home appreciates $12,000 the first twelve months, giving a 120 percent internal rate of return on the initial $10,000 investment with no tax liability. This certainly is a lot of value.

Consider the other nontangible values the house gives off. Go back and consider the list of memories listed above. Memories cannot be measured in dollars and cents. The return on this initial investment is infinite. The chance of losing these memories is very low.

Say the stock you purchased also had a growth of 6 percent. Your investment grows $600, of which you will pay capital gains taxes on. What other value other than the dollar does your stock investment bring? Perhaps it may bring a little security for future use if it continues to grow.

In this book, we are considering how to become a better fiscal steward of that which God has given us financially to manage. You decide which option is a better investment choice. Many people try to convince us how bad mortgages are—more so today as the mortgage markets reveal major flaws over the last several years.

These people, often of the baby boomer or depression generations, talk of mortgages as the worst possible things a person could have. Well, you've just seen above how a mortgage can leverage a much greater return for your hard-earned dollar. But let's consider the opposition to the mortgage.

During the Great Depression, people bought stock on "margin" for 10 cents on the dollar. Margin is a stock term for loans. When the market crashed in October, 1929, the brokerages called these margin loans due. When people went to the bank for money, the banks ran out of money, leaving people without a way to pay these debts to the stock market.

In order to raise money to pay the people, banks called their mortgages loans due. Anyone who had a mortgage loan was expected to pay in full or lose their homes. Companies lost millions of dollars and laid off millions of people, who were now expected to pay off a mortgage. Right. So the banks had millions of homes they now couldn't sell to a population of jobless people.

People who did not have a mortgage saw this and praised God for not letting the bank "take their home." A new tradition was born. Get rid of the mortgage as fast as possible so the bank can't take the home back.

Good news, my friends. The laws have changed. It is illegal for banks to call mortgages due if payments are being made according to the loan agreement.

As a result of this thinking, many financial pitfalls have come over us. The banks still market paying off the note early. They show how to make additional payments to "save money" on long-term interest. Many people continue to send extra money to the bank to pay down the mortgage while carrying short-term debts like car loans and credit cards.

I am a fan of having no mortgage. I am also a fan of having a mortgage as long as I can and using the bank's money to leverage my growing asset rather than my own money.

I don't believe paying the mortgage off is the most important financial goal. I believe that this is one of the last steps to a sound financial plan after eliminating all other consumer debts and securing a strong future savings plan.

Tax Advantages

So let's consider a couple of other factors of importance when looking at mortgage loans.

Some keys in gaining good financing options are as follows. When you are getting ready to buy a home, you will probably need to talk with a mortgage professional to set up the financing. There are many other ways to purchase a home; but for the purpose of our study here, we'll assume a mortgage from a traditional lending source like a bank or mortgage broker.

When the closing takes place on the home, some of the fees, called *discount points* or *origination points*, paid to the lender are tax-deductible items. Also, the pre-paid interest paid at closing is tax deductible. These are good things to keep in mind since they will save you a portion on your tax bill in April. Be sure to keep copies of the HUD1 settlement statement to document these items. A good lender will provide a copy of this to you in January, but it is not mandatory that they do so.

Another deduction related to owning your home the IRS allows you is the tax you pay for your property. Each year, the county charges property taxes to raise money for schools, roads, hospitals, etc. to support the local infrastructure of the community.

The government is excited to offer homeowners tax advantages due to the affect homeownership has on the overall economy. Consider the impact of buying a home. Think of the jobs created to build the home, deliver the materials, sell the materials, sell the home, the carpet, the drapes, the blinds, the plumbing, the electric, etc. Think about Home Depot and Lowe's shortly after purchase. Many home buyers spend thousands of dollars on furniture, paint, hardware, landscaping, and the list goes on. The IRS is very happy to give these tax breaks.

When you buy, the interest you pay on your owner-occupied home loan is also tax deductible for most families. There will be some variance depending on each individual tax picture. It is important that you consult a qualified tax preparer who can advise you about your tax situation. Generally, many people enjoy the interest deduction from their tax bill.

The thirty-year mortgage you have on your home is front-loaded, meaning the interest is collected at the beginning and the principal is paid toward the end of the thirty-year term. A typical $100,000 home loan at 6 percent will have approximately $500 per month applied to interest or $6,000 per year applied in interest. This interest will reduce your tax bill, depending upon the tax bracket you fall in. For many families, the mortgage interest is the only deduction they have on their taxes. It is a great advantage to consider.

Now, I would also like to advise you that taking out a mortgage for the purpose of getting a tax deduction is not necessarily advisable. The deduction of $6,000, as outlined above, at 25 percent tax bracket will save you approximately $1,500 on your tax bill. So do the math. Fifteen hundred dollars less in taxes means $4,500 in interest bill. From where I sit, $4,500 is still a bigger number than $1,500.

As long as the rest of your financial house is in order (consult a qualified advisor), eliminating your mortgage is beneficial. These are much more advanced strategies that go beyond the scope of this text.

It is important to note that the tax advantages of buying a home outweigh the absolute loss of renting and throwing money at a landlord. If you are able to buy a home, the advantages are great.

So Why Rent?

Buying a home is a very personal experience. It will be different for every family. When considering buying versus renting, there are factors to consider.

How long will you need to reside in the home? Will your job be relocating you in the short term (less than two years)?

What is your risk tolerance? Many people consider buying a home a risky purchase. Reduce your risk by educating yourself on the different aspects that you consider risky. Many believe that real estate is too volatile, and you may lose money in your investment. Yes, this is true. Be sure to weigh against the prospect of the guaranteed loss of renting. With rent, you are guaranteed every month to write a check that you will absolutely never see again. So before using risk as a reason not to buy, make sure you know what you are comparing.

Can you afford the monthly payments? Many times, buying a home works out to be less costly than renting, but buying has other costs that renting does not have, like maintenance costs, utilities are charged differently, decorating you would not do in a rental, etc. Don't be naïve, thinking that only the payments need to be considered.

Many lenders will lend far more than you can actually afford based on your lifestyle. For example, many times a buyer can "qualify" for 45 percent or more of their gross income. Does this mean they should purchase a home that eats up more than half of their income? Remember that the IRS, state, and health care company is getting about 32 percent every paycheck. That only leaves 23 cents out of every dollar to pay utilities, food, gas in the car, phone, entertainment, etc.

This is the most overlooked part of buying a home. Before sitting down with a lender, *know your numbers*. Do you know how much you can pay for a house every month? If you don't know how to manage your budget, you certainly don't need to buy *yet*. Spend the time necessary to get your financial house in order before you try to add the responsibility of a house only you are responsible for. No one else can bail you out if you get over your head (although the government is trying).

What are your fears of owning a home? I don't believe that fear is ever a reason to not do something. Fear is merely the product of limited knowledge. Today, we have access to more information in twenty-four hours than our depression era grandparents had in their entire adult lives. Use the tools and resources you have available to get educated about your decision.

There are plenty of people who can and will help you make your decision. Just keep in mind that this is *your* decision. You have to live with the choice you make. There is no amount of education that is too much on this subject. Don't allow your emotions to take the front seat on this decision.

If you've gone through these questions and others in making your decision and still feel that renting is right for you, then by all means, renting is right for you. Personally, I do not plan on renting in my lifetime due to the knowledge I now possess on the subject. But my plans may change based on things I can't yet see.

Why Did We Buy?

I told you at the beginning of this chapter that I once held the belief that buying a home was ungodly in some way. When I was single, I saw that Jesus didn't have a home or a "place to lay his head" and decided that I also needed to live like this. My beliefs about the subject ran so deep that I nearly declined my career in mortgages for *fear* of making too much money.

The first home we bought came eighteen months after we were married. I was very confident early on in our marriage that, as a family man, renting was not the best way to go. Now keep in mind that we lived in a dumpy little two-bedroom townhouse that we could barely afford at $410 per month in 1999. The carpet was so worn in spots that you could see the backing tape through the nap. There were tiles missing or broken in the kitchen. There was a hole in the wall inside one of the floor cabinets in our kitchen. We kept camping gear in that "roach and rat" invitation. It was quite the home.

I got the idea that we should buy when an older woman across the street was thinking of selling and moving in with her kids. The problem was that we could not afford her home. Oh, how I wanted it though. I would drive by every day thinking, *Someday, we will have our house.*

After a year of debate, Belinda and I decided to go for it. Our credit was shot, and we had no money for a down payment. Our oldest daughter was just born, so Belinda wasn't working. I was getting ready to start school full-time in a couple of months, cutting my work hours to twenty per week.

We were scared out of our minds, but I knew that we still had to live somewhere and pay someone something. We were throwing money away. It took us a couple of months. We made offers on four homes before one was finally accepted. It was the first house we looked at. It was $5,000 over the top of our price range. (On a $59,000 house, $5,000 is nearly 10 percent of the asking price.) The seller agreed to come down on the price, so we moved in a week after my school semester started.

Our new house payment was about $75 more than we were currently paying in rent. How the heck was that going to work out? To this day, I don't know how we did it, but we were never late. We never went without food.

Life for us changed dramatically. I became manager of the bank where I worked, and Belinda ended up going back to work. Our income grew quite a bit during those days.

Even though we stretched ourselves, the Lord provided along the way; and that home holds many memories for us. I will go back and buy that home as a rental one of these days because that is where it all began for us. As for now, we are grateful for all of the memories the Lord has given us in all three of our homes.

It was nine years ago when we bought our first home. Today, we can't imagine not owning a home. We pray that our home is a great blessing to our family and to those the Lord places in our lives. We have been referred to as Hotel Christensen on more than one occasion. We truly believe that our home is an extension of our ministry and a great tool to be used for impacting others for the Lord.

I do know the fears. Don't do anything that would ever jeopardize your relationship with the Lord. A home is never something that should be considered worldly. We live in the world, as Jesus prayed in John 17. As a part of the world, everything we have and do is worldly. All we can do is take what we have and use it to honor our God and bless one another as he would have us do.

My prayers are with you as you make this very important decision in your lives. I pray that your decision honors the Lord and that he blesses your desires.

Passing on Legacy

> Go to the ant, you sluggard; consider its ways and be wise! It has no commander, no overseer or ruler, yet it stores its provisions in summer and gathers food at harvest. A little sleep a little slumber, a little folding of the hands to rest—and poverty will come on you like a bandit and scarcity like an armed man.
>
> Proverbs 6:6–11 (NIV)

We're coming to an end in our lesson. Pay very close attention to this one, as legacy is what our lives are about. In the previous chapter of lifestyle, we discussed the parable of the prodigal son who squandered his inheritance. If the son had an inheritance to squander, it was due to the father having an inheritance to give.

Do you remember Jacob and Esau? Jacob deceived Esau to gain the blessing and inheritance of the father.

What about the promise Peter makes for us, our children, and for those who are far off (Acts 2:39,)?

Make no mistake. God's heart of leaving a legacy is very important indeed. The entire gospel is about making known his plans for us while he is gone. In fact, the very salvation of God is described as our inheritance kept for us in heaven (1 Peter 1:4). Yes, we are to be left behind, so let's be clear about legacy. Jesus left us lessons and blessings to live. We too should do the same for those we leave behind.

As long as we are taken before Jesus returns, our families and children will be left behind with memories of us. What will they hold dear to them? Will they remember us for, our money or the life lessons we taught them?

Have you ever written your own eulogy? Do you know what it is you want those closest to you to say about you when you are gone? Think about this for a moment. I'll use myself as example.

Let's say I am taken prematurely. What will my family remember me for? Will my children pass on the lessons I taught them? Will my wife be able to maintain the education of our children as we planned because I set them up financially? Will the impact I left in the lives of the people I touched be in vain, or will it be with great effect? Was my life like dropping a pebble in sand or in water? Will there be ripples?

The purpose of this book is to discuss God's intent for us financially. So, in this final chapter, let's discuss the importance of leaving behind a legacy for those we love. First, we must define *legacy*.

Going back to Mr. Webster, *legacy* is simply: 1. money or property bequeathed by a will or 2. something handed down from an ancestor or from the past.

In this chapter, we will discuss both. Let's start with our discussion on money and then we will follow with oral tradition or lessons from our past. Both of these are like the wings of an airplane. It's important to pass both to those we love. One without the other could lead to a disaster.

Look at Paris Hilton as an example. Heiress to the great Hilton fortune, but she has no manners in treating people. It is unfortunate when thinking of all the good that she could do to help the world; but instead, she is too concerned with her party lifestyle.

Money

> A good man leaves an inheritance to his grandchildren, but the sinner's wealth is stored up for the righteous.
>
> Proverbs 13:22 (NIV)

When we play games, we look for the rich relative who left us money. Have you ever known anyone who received an inheritance? Unfortunately, money left for a grandchild or child who has no training on what to do with it is squandered, like the unfortunate prodigal son.

There are many things to consider when setting up your estate. I will not go into a lengthy description of the estate due to legalities of which I am not licensed to advise. I will, however, express a high recommendation to take the time to gain the education and knowledge necessary to your personal scenario. Every person will have a completely different need in establishing their estate. Seek out counsel appropriately, and do not trust every Tom, Dick, or Harry to advise you in this.

Keep in mind that not all "advisers" have your best

interests in mind. Many advisers are trying to get some of your children's inheritance for themselves. There are many advisers out there who will try to set up a trust or estate plan for you when you do not need one. Not everyone needs these, but many will. If you've planned wisely and applied many of the principles of this book, along with other very wise plans, you may be in a very good position to establish a trust or estate plan.

Also, a will may or may not be the best way to protect what you've worked your entire life to build for your family. Again, seek out knowledgeable counsel to advise you in your personal situation.

Let's take a look now at different types of Life Insurance.

Life Insurance

When buying life insurance, be aware of the many scams out there trying to hook you into a program that is not best for the level of asset protection you need.

There are many different flavors of life insurance. Keep in mind, however, that there are only two types of life insurance protection: (1) term and (2) cash value insurance. Both have important roles, but both are not practical for every family. There are many different variations within each family of insurance, so let's take a look at these briefly.

- *Term insurance*: This is as easy as it gets when considering an insurance product. It is called term insurance because the premiums you are paying protect you for a timeframe or "term" that is predetermined when you set this up. If you were to die while the policy is in effect, the beneficiary receives the face value of the policy. There is nothing fancy about this. The younger you are, the more affordable the premiums.

- *Whole life insurance*: Commonly called "cash value" or "permanent life insurance." There is no term in place. As long as you continue to pay the premium, this policy will follow your life as you grow older. As you pay your premiums, part of the money pays the agent's commission and the company's administration costs each time you renew; and the other part goes into a reserve account set aside as "cash value." After a few years pass, the reserve account grows to have a "cash value" that begins to build tax-free. This money can be drawn against several different ways. You can draw against the money by 1) borrowing against it while the policy is still in force, 2) directing the company to use it to purchase a paid up policy of the same amount, 3) directing the company to pay the policy premiums, or 4) surrendering the policy and taking the cash out. If you die while the policy is still in effect, the beneficiary will receive the "face value" of the policy, less any loans against the policy.

The age-old question that many have debated in the insurance world is, "Why wouldn't I buy a term policy and control my investment separately?"

These are important questions that you should answer. In leaving a legacy, the most important thing to consider is how your family will be protected in the event that you are no longer with them. Plan and prepare for them if you are called home.

In the case of my wife and me, it is important that she be able to continue home schooling our children if I am gone. That means that we need adequate protection to maintain that lifestyle in my absence. Your goals may be different; but nonetheless, plan for your family goals.

If you haven't laid out any goals for your family, start here. If you have, you're already ahead of 90 percent of Americans.

Seek out a good insurance advisor who will advise you in your best interest, not the advisor's best interest. Check with friends, family, and others you trust for their recommendation of who to talk with about this important protection.

Too many times, I've seen young, single mothers who lost their husbands who did not protect their families' future because they would be around for a long time. Then there was a diagnosis of a disease like cancer or a car accident that took them suddenly in their youth. Take time to plan. This is important.

Another important area to consider when planning for your family's financial future is to consider a will or trust.

Wills and Trusts

- *Wills*: A will is a legal document used to determine the deceased person's "Last Will and Testament" for how he would like his personal possessions and assets divided. It also determines how the deceased would like his children cared for in his/her absence. This can be a very sobering act to sit and determine how you would like your estate divided up; but since you will not be able to advise upon your death, a will tells the courts how to manage your estate after your death. There are many different types of wills as well as ways to set them up. Software programs, online programs, and even "Wills while you wait" kind of "fast food" fashion are available to help you set these up. Be careful. This is not an area you want to "save money" on by using less than adequate programs. Take the time to carefully plan your will with a qualified legal advisor who can help you understand the process beyond your life here. This will ensure that your family will not have to face unnecessary legal problems in the event of your death.

- *Trusts*: A trust is an arrangement in which you legally transfer your assets to an entity with its own tax identification number with legal agreements set up by you and an attorney to be administered by an individual or institution for a beneficiary. These entities can be set up while you are still alive, with you as the managing administrator or "trustee" with specific designations or assignments of a new trustee in the event of your death. In conjunction with a will, a trust can potentially keep the legal battle very simple after a death since the trust is a legal entity that owns the assets, not the person who died. Again, be sure to visit with a qualified legal advisor who can help you set this up. Not everyone needs a trust. There are many lawyers out there who will take advantage of a person,

> stating that they need a trust when they don't have any assets to protect. Setting up a trust can be costly and requires regular maintenance as your life and assets change.

Another way to leave a financial legacy for your family when you leave this world is to establish a good Estate Plan.

Estate Plans

An estate plan may only be necessary if you start to realize more than $500,000 in assets. Even a $500,000 estate is not a big estate. The more assets you have in your estate when you die, the more estate tax the IRS can get their hands on. There are limitations; so if you currently don't have a net worth of at least half a million, don't worry about this step in your planning. If you do have at least $500,000 in net worth, run, don't walk to a good estate attorney and tax accountant to find out how you can set up your estate to preserve and protect it from unnecessary taxes and fees when you transfer the estate to your beneficiaries. There are all kinds of rumors out there of what you can and can't do. Seek professional help, not your friendly banker, a legal advisor who is qualified in estate planning.

I was a banker for many years. Trust me when I say that your banker doesn't know what he is talking about. I don't care how nice he is. The banks don't train the folks in the lobby who manage your accounts how to protect an estate. Now don't get me wrong. I advised plenty of people with very bad advice. At the time, I thought I was giving very good advice. Later, I found out I set many of my clients up for bad situations. Now I pray that these folks got better advice later. That was many years ago. The point is that your banker wants to help you when you ask, but just because he answers doesn't mean he's got the legal background to advise you.

I was a banker for many years, from age twenty-two to twenty-six. I also managed a very large national bank with many millions of dollars of assets and eighteen employees when I was twenty-seven years old with no college degree. I can assure you that it doesn't take a college or legal degree to give out financial advice in our country. Be careful who you take your advice from.

The final thing I want to say about leaving a financial legacy behind is that you've worked incredibly hard learning how to manage your cash flow, buying assets rather than liabilities, and planning for a future with very limited liabilities. Why would you not take the extra time to protect this legacy for the next generation?

Oral Traditions and Lessons from Your Past

> I am now going the way of all the earth, and you know with all your heart and all your soul that none of the good promises the Lord your God made to you has failed. Everything was fulfilled for you; not one promise has failed.
>
> Joshua 23:14 (NIV)

We've looked at what it takes to protect your financial assets. Now let's take a look at the more important piece of the puzzle. One thing I've learned is that money comes and money goes. As Sir Issac Newton found out, what goes up must come down. I tell you that money has its own set of laws associated with it as well.

The most important thing you can do to ensure a legacy is teach your children how money works the way you've learned. Some of the biggest lessons I learned growing up included:

- It's no one's business how much money you make.
- What do you think, that money grows on trees?
- No. We can't afford that.
- No. We're on a budget.
- Save your money. Put it in the bank.
- Trust your banker. He'll help you make smart decisions.
- Shop around and "save" money.
- Go to college, work hard, and get a good job.
- Look for a company with good benefits.
- Job security (What does that even mean any-more?)

There are countless other lessons we learned growing up. If you think about it, these all have limitations, with very little hope for a future.

Our world is changing, so don't think you're educating your children on these changes. If you're not taking the time to teach them, don't worry. The marketing and advertisers for major corporations are teaching your children how to save money. The key to saving is by spending money at their stores or on their products. We live in a nation of heavy consumption. Our marketing agencies have done an amazing job at creating a society where entitlement rules.

Did you know that Santa Clause and the Christmas tree were actually institutionalized by advertisers and marketers? The jolly, red-suited Santa actually came on the scene as an icon through the genius of Coca-Cola in the 1930s. Rudolph the Red-nosed Reindeer was a story that a department store executive created to attract kids whose parents would buy more toys for their children.

The commercialization of Christmas is the only time of the year when we, as Americans, feel compelled to spend money to give. Thank you, Mr. Advertiser, for this legacy of entitlement. Microwave ovens, instant popcorn, fast food, debit cards, credit cards, instant cash, cash advances, buy now pay later, get rich quick, you deserve it…

Think about the financial mistakes you've made in your life, and ask what you're doing to stop your children from making the same mistakes. There are many books out today that teach how to teach our kids financial responsibility. Financial IQ is much more important than intellectual IQ. You can read and be as smart in trivia as you like; but if you can't keep food on the table, what good is it?

Our world is rapidly changing, and we have an enemy among us, wishing to devour us. Satan is cunning. He is deceiving in many ways. We are all sheep among wolves. We no longer live in the industrial age.

Wake up and realize that *now* is the time to "train a

youth about the way he should go; even when he is old he will not depart from it," (Proverbs 22:6, NIV).

The Internet is full of all kinds of information, both good and bad. If you don't take the time to educate yourself in these matters, your children will reveal the true legacy that you left behind by the ways you trained them or didn't.

If you're not training them, someone is. Don't be naïve.

If you skip this part, you can leave millions behind for your children who will squander it due to the lack of financial IQ you left behind for them to manage it.

If you leave them with a financial IQ, you can leave them no money and they will be just fine. Think about the Chinese Proverb that says, "You can give a man a fish and feed him for a day, or you can teach a man to fish and feed him for a lifetime." You decide what type of legacy you'd like to leave behind.

With that, I'm going to leave you with my personal eulogy that I wrote a few years ago. This is the way I want to be remembered as I leave this world. I do hope that I live my life in a way to not only accomplish this but also to leave a lasting legacy that honors God in what he has done in my life.

May God bless you in all of your endeavors. You're always in my prayers.

I would love to hear from you about how this book has made a difference in your life. You can send me an e-mail at joshua@considertheantonline.com.

Thank you for your support. One last request I have is to share this message with as many as you know. I truly believe that this message is important and needs to get out to many. A pebble in a pond has many ripples. You can make a difference in someone's life and change it forever!

I'll close with this final thought. Thank you for reading. I do pray that this has been a blessing in your life.

My Eulogy

Joshua was a man of integrity, truth, dedication, devotion, and passion. He followed through on the promises he made in his life, starting with his devotion to Christ. He lived a life of complete devotion to Christ, making no apologies. He was never ashamed of that allegiance. His devotion to Belinda was characterized by the life of love that he gave her. He went out of his way to make sure that she knew his love for her. He was committed to building a life of memories and impact as they lived their partnership, their friendship, and their love. He was a man known for his undying love for his children, committed in every way to that which would give them the fullest life possible, equipping them with everything they would need for their success in the life to follow his own. Joshua is known and will be remembered for his love. He is a forgiven man that lived a forgiven life and offered love to the world out of the love that he received from the Father. He was passionate about doing that which would add the most value to the lives of the people he touched. Joshua truly lived his life. "He has showed you, O Man, what is good. And what does the Lord require of you? To act justly and to love mercy and to walk humbly with your God…" (Micah 6:8, NIV). "But as for me and my household, we will serve the Lord," (Joshua 24:15, NIV). Joshua lived these passages and many more, as he always kept his eyes on the cross of reconciliation to the Father and followed in the steps of Jesus' love.

Appendix A

What Have I Been Given?

During this exercise, please take some time to examine the blessings that God has given you. This is a very essential part to understanding stewardship. If you don't know what God has placed you in charge of, you won't be able to manage it well.

Shelter

Describe where you live.

____

____

____

Do you rent, or do you own?

____

What area of town do you live in?

____

Are you cold at night?

____

Describe your bed.

____

____

____

Food

Describe your pantry.

____

____

____

Describe your meals today.

____

____

____

Describe your snacks today.

____

____

____

Describe the last time you went without a meal. (How long?)

____

____

____

Describe your typical shopping list.

____

____

____

What is your favorite meal? When did you have it last?

____

____

____

Relationships

Do you have a significant other?

____

Describe your favorite relationship. (Not your significant other.)

____

____

____

Do you have children?

____

Are your parents/grand parents still living?

____

Do you ever grumble or complain about your relationships?

____

Describe your biggest complaint.

____

____

____

Education

Describe your highest level of education.

Can you read?

Write?

Do you?

Have you earned the highest level of education you wish to receive?

Explain.

Employment

Describe your current job status.

____

____

____

Do you like your job?

____

Describe your attitude while working.

____

____

____

Describe your compensation.

____

____

____

Assets

Describe how much you have in the following types of accounts…

Checking:

____

Savings:

____

Money Mkt:

____

CD:

____

IRA:

____

401k:

____

Investments

____

Describe any real estate you own.
Primary Home
Value:

____

Loan:

____

Purchase Price:

____

How long:

____

Rental Home
Value:

____

Loan:

____

Purchase Price:

____

How long:

____

Other Real Estate
Value:

____

Loan:

____

Purchase Price:

____

How long:

____

Describe your cars.
Model:

____

Year:

____

Make:

____

Value:

____

Purchase Price:

____

How long:

____

New or used:

____

Amount owed:

____

Describe your home furnishings.

____

____

____

____

____

Describe your electronics.

Describe any tools you have.

Describe your exercise equipment.

Talents

Describe your top three talents or strengths.

1. ____________________

2. ____________________

3. ____________________

Describe how you are using these talents in your life.

____

____

____

Describe what you are doing to improve your talents.

____

____

____

Where did all these things come from?

____

____

____

Do you believe it?

____

Describe how your life reflects this conviction.

____

____

____

____

____

____

Appendix B

Getting Ready for the Practicals

By this point, you should have completed the following items:

1. What I've Been Given Assessment
2. Answered how you are developing each area of the assessment and how you are caring for each area
3. Read the book of Proverbs

Going into the practical application, please prepare the following items.

1. Personal Monthly Budget (in the format you use)
    A. Break down your gross income, taxes, health care, 401k, etc.
    B. List your net income (what you bring home)

C. What are your variable monthly bills (utilities, credit cards, etc. that change from month to month)?

D. What are your fixed monthly bills (rent/mortgage, contribution, car, etc. that does not change from month to month)

E. How much do you give in contribution monthly?

2. What needs to happen in your practical application? What are your biggest three goals?

A. ______________________________

____

____

B. ______________________________

____

____

C. ______________________________

____

____

3. Create an asset ledger (in your own format)

A. List all liquid bank accounts

B. List all CDs

C. List retirement accounts

D. List investment accounts (stocks, mutual funds)

E. List any government bonds (series EE)

4. What are your top three asset goals?

A. ____________________

____

____

B. ____________________

____

____

C. ____________________

____

____

5. How much are you currently saving monthly?

$ ____________________

6. How much would you like to have in savings?

$ ____________________

7. Why is reaching this goal important to you?

____

____

____

8. If you reach this goal, describe what would this mean for you or your family.

____

____

____

Appendix C

Recommended Reading List

Kick Your Excuses Goodbye! by Rene Godefroy

How to Win Friends and Influence People by Dale Carnegie

The Richest Man In Babylon by George S. Clason

How to Be Rich by J. Paul Getty

Ordinary People, Extraordinary Wealth by Ric Edelman

New Rules of Money by Ric Edelman

Think and Grow Rich by Napoleon Hill

The Rules of Money by Templar

The Richest man Who Ever Lived by Steven Scott

Let Your Life Speak by Palmer

The Millionaire Next Door by Stanley/Danko

Secrets of the Millionaire Mind by T. Harv Eker

7 *Habits of Highly Effective P*eople by Stephen Covey

The Financial Peace Planner by Dave Ramsey

Rich Dad, Poor Dad by Robert Kiyosaki

Cash Flow Quadrant by Robert Kiyosaki

Missed Fortune 101 by Douglas Andrew

Appendix D

Net Worth Statement

Category

Assets

Cash ______________________

Savings Accounts ______________________

Checking Accounts ______________________

Certificates of Deposit ______________________

Money Market Accounts ______________________

Money Owed to Me (utility/rent deposits) ______________________

Life Insurance (Cash Value) ______________________

Stocks ______________________

Bonds	______
Mutual Funds	______
Other Investments	______
IRA	______
SEP Accounts	______
Keogh Accounts	______
401(k) or 403 (b)	______
Other Retirement	______
Mkt Value (Home)	______
Mkt Value (other Real Estate)	______
Cars & Trucks (Blue Book)	______
Other Vehicles	______
Jewelry and Collectibles	______
Personal Property	______
Other Misc. Assets	______
Total Assets	______

Liabilities

Mortgages ____________________

Auto Loans ____________________

Credit Card Balances ____________________

Home Equity Loans ____________________

Student Loans ____________________

Other Loans ____________________

Real Estate Taxes ____________________

Income Taxes ____________________

Other Taxes ____________________

Other Misc. Debt ____________________

Total Liabilities ____________________

____

Assets $ ____________________

- Liabilities $ ____________________

=Net Worth $ ____________________

Your net worth statement is a snapshot of your financial health on any given day you fill it in with current numbers. It tells you in dollars and cents what you are worth.

This is a good tool to measure your financial health and overall fiscal stewardship before God.

Appendix E

The Debt Snowball

List your debts in order, with the smallest payoff or balance first. Do not be concerned with interest rates or terms unless two debts have similar payoffs; then list the higher interest rate debt first. Paying the little debts off first gives you quick feedback, and you are more likely to stay with the plan.

Redo this sheet each time you pay off a debt so that you can see how close you are getting to freedom. Keep the old sheets to wallpaper the bathroom in your new debt-free house. The "new payment" is found by adding all the payments on the debts listed above that item to the payment you are working on, so you have compounding payments that will get you out of debt very quickly. "Payments remaining" is the number of payments remaining when you get down the snowball to that item. "Cumulative payments" is the total payments needed, including the snowball, to pay off that item. In other words, this is your running total for "payments remaining."

Countdown to Freedom

Date: ______________________

Item Payoff	Total Payment	Minimum Payment	New Payment	Payment Remaining	Cumulative Payments

Appendix F

Your Personal Eulogy

We want to hear from you. Please send your comments to review@considertheantonline.com. Thank you.

Requests for information should be addressed to:
Consider the Ant Ministries
PO Box 66048, Albuquerque, NM 87193